rituals

for

every day

For our teachers

rituals

for

every day

nadia narain
&
katia narain phillips

CONTENTS

RITUALS

What do you think of when you hear the word ritual? We find some people are intrigued and even excited by the idea of a ritual, and ready to try anything, however strange it may sound at first. Cover myself in jasmine oil to attract love? Sure, why not? Others are worried it means getting involved in some kind of witchy pagan seance, and the very idea makes them want to freak out.

Don't worry, sometimes the thought of a ritual makes us want to roll our eyes, too. We're not here to tell you that you must embrace a whole world of mysticism, or that you should carve out hours of your time for casting spells (unless you want to!). And we're not going to make you buy a special juju kit that you'd be embarrassed for your friends to see.

For us, a ritual is a simple way of learning to celebrate the small things in life. It's a way of making ordinary things special, and special things extra special.

Rituals are a way of acknowledging and honouring our emotions and experiences, and they can give us a safe place to lay down some of our more difficult feelings so that we don't feel suffocated by them.

One message that we hear time and again when running our self-care workshops is that people recognise the need to slow down and create more space in their lives, but they're just not sure how to do it. We hope this book will give you some easy-to-follow advice on how simple rituals can help you press the pause button on the pace of modern life.

If the idea of a ritual seems intimidating or off-putting to you, think of the joyous rituals that all cultures share around the ideas of birth, marriage or festivals. At their best, these rituals give us a framework within which we can explore ideas of change and growth; we pause to note the passing of time, and to celebrate it. Even the most passionate atheist will have been to a birthday party or a New Year's Eve celebration, without necessarily recognising either as a ritual.

A ritual can also support you in difficult times. If you have ever attended the funeral of a loved one, you will know that the ancient rituals around death can be a source of deep comfort when the idea of making decisions feels overwhelming.

On the crazy busy treadmill of modern life, we still embrace the rituals that mark the big life events such as funerals, weddings and births, but many of us seem to have lost the small moments of reflection and ceremony from the everyday. We believe that life without reflection and contemplation is a recipe for dissatisfaction and burnout.

Bringing rituals into your daily life can help you move through busy times in a way that feels graceful and deliberate, instead of rushed and routine. We like to think of our suggested rituals as a series of recipes that can show you how to bring some sweetness back into your day.

WHAT IS A RITUAL ANYWAY?

Some of our rituals are so simple we can explain them in a sentence, while others are more involved, with specific steps and instructions. What all of them share, though, is a sense of learning to live your life with purpose and intention.

A ritual can be whatever you want it to be, but we believe that all rituals involve three stages:

PAUSE to acknowledge where you are, how you feel, and what is going on in this moment.

PAY ATTENTION to your emotions, to your breathing, to any sensations in your body.

SET YOUR INTENTION – are you looking for peace? Energy? Acceptance? Change? Be clear in your intention.

It really can be as simple as that – no candles, no incense, no sitting cross-legged on a meditation cushion. But the effect of even such a simple ritual can be profound.

A ritual should not be rushed, but it doesn't have to take up a lot of time either. We believe a ritual should give you a deeper sense of wellbeing, and of connection to the world around you. Think of it as helping to bring a little magic into the mundane.

We also love the idea of rituals that can be passed down through generations, or given as gifts to help bring a little stillness to someone else's life, so we've included some of those here.

So the basis of a ritual as we define it is incredibly simple, and everything else is an add-on. We're going to offer suggestions for some more detailed rituals throughout this book, but you can take or leave these.

The hippy in us loves a crystal and an essential oil, so we use these often, but you don't have to. Just keep coming back to the reminder to pause, pay attention and set your intention, and you're already practising and refining your own ritual.

Try to remember that a ritual is here to serve you and support you, not the other way around. If you feel yourself getting too attached to any ritual   one from this book, or from elsewhere – remind yourself that a ritual is about honouring your experience, not dictating it.

THIS ALL SOUNDS GREAT, BUT WHO HAS THE TIME?

Far from taking up time, we believe that embracing the gentle power of rituals will help you to *make* time.

We all have twenty-four hours in each day. That's everyone from Barack Obama to the Dalai Lama to you. And of course some days are going to be more hectic and others calmer, but in every single day you have a choice about how you use your time.

When people say to us that they don't have time to slow down, what they're really saying is that they're not making it a priority. You have to make a positive choice to bring moments of stillness and harmony into your own life – no one else will do it for you!

Begin to notice the habits that waste your time and make you feel depleted, then ask yourself if you can use that time more productively.

We've learned that whenever we rush around thinking we don't have time for those little pockets of calm – whether that's meditation, walking or just sitting still – life seems to speed up and come at us harder than ever.

There is a famous Zen saying that you should meditate every morning for twenty minutes, unless you are really busy, in which case you should meditate for an hour. Because it is in those frantic moments that we most need a framework that will bring us to a place of peace.

Taking responsibility for slowing down and looking after yourself will make life feel more spacious.

WHAT IS THE DIFFERENCE BETWEEN A HABIT AND A RITUAL?

It's important to make a distinction between a habit, which is an action that we perform automatically, without thinking of it, and a ritual, which we perform with attention and intention.

HABIT	RITUAL
Eating on the run	Giving thanks before you eat
Scrolling through social media	Reading an inspirational book
Grabbing a takeaway croissant	Sitting down to a homemade breakfast
Switching on the TV every night	Writing in a gratitude journal

Good habits can enhance our lives, and we totally believe in maintaining the habits that keep us strong, healthy and happy. But don't get us wrong, you don't have to replace every daily habit with a carefully considered ritual – no one has time for that.

What you can do, though, is turn a habit into a super simple ritual just by changing the intention behind it.

So instead of drinking your tea while you're getting dressed in the morning, try making a small ceremony out of it. Use loose-leaf tea, warm the teapot, brew the leaves for the perfect length of time and enjoy your cup in a moment of peace before the day begins. It's the attention to detail and the awareness of the moment that separates the habit from the ritual.

If you feel you don't have time to practise a ritual, start with very simple ones, linked to the actions you already do each day. Can you use the time while you're brushing your teeth to set your intention for the day ahead? Can you add a drop of essential oil to your moisturiser – maybe lavender for calm – to reflect how you're feeling, or how you want to feel?

The beneficial effect of these small rituals is cumulative – the more often you practise them, the more they help you reach a place where you feel safe and supported, regardless of what else might be happening in your life.

Just as creating good habits requires discipline, feeling the benefit from the practise of rituals will take time. The first time you practise a ritual it may feel weird and uncomfortable, the second time you're maybe getting used to it, the third time it feels better.

This book is full of ideas for rituals that have worked for us and the people we work with. See what inspires you, and feel free to play with all of these ideas and shape them into something that really resonates with you.

Remember that a ritual can turn into a habit if you're not paying attention to it. Try not to let your rituals become stale – keep them fresh and meaningful so that you're fully engaged and not just going through the motions.

WHAT IF I'M NOT RELIGIOUS?

Our background is pretty eclectic – our mother is South African, our father Indian, and we were born and raised in Hong Kong before we both settled in London. We travelled widely from a young age, and between Nadia living on an ashram and studying Buddhism, and Katia converting to Judaism when she got married, we think of ourselves these days as a happy mishmash of cultures and traditions.

We're lucky to have experienced many different rituals over the years, and as well as practising the familiar ones we know and love, our background means we are always open to adopting new rituals and adapting them to enhance and enrich our lives.

Whether you are religious, spiritual or firmly atheist, it's our belief that everyone is searching for meaning in their life. You might look for that meaning through work or relationships or creative expression; everyone's different.

In our experience, the only way you can begin to understand what brings meaning to your own life is to get slow and quiet and still, and to listen. Regardless of your religion, or lack of it, stillness will have the answer. And rituals can help you to find that stillness.

We hope that some of these rituals will resonate with you. We've tried to give pretty clear guidance, but we'd like you to take our ideas as inspiration rather than strict instruction.

We adapt these rituals all the time, and so should you.

Let rituals bring you back to yourself.

beginning

'This being human is a guest house.
Every morning a new arrival.' *Rumi*

What does a beginning feel like to you?

For us it's a step into that space when something fresh and new begins to grow. Beginnings can be both exciting and scary, and we've found they often come to us at the end of a really hard time, like a light at the end of the tunnel. When you're feeling overwhelmed by starting over, it can help to remind yourself that the end of one thing may mean the beginning of something better.

A beginning can be as big as a new home or relationship, or as small as the start of a new day, or even a new hour. The great thing about beginnings is that you can make a fresh start at any time.

It can be hard to know when we're at the beginning of something – often we're in the middle before we realise we've started something new. But it's never too late to pause and reflect on the beginning – even if it has passed.

Just like the seasons, we humans have times of growth and change, and we have times of hibernation and restoration. Yours may match up with the seasons themselves or they may not; we know some people who feel sad in the summer and truly love winter.

Spring may be the time to sow seeds (be it literally or metaphorically) but trust your intuition and begin your beginnings when the time feels right to you, rather than according to the calendar.

Now let's begin.

YOUR MORNING

How you start your morning has such an impact on the rest of your day. Think of those mornings where you sleep through your alarm and have to rush to get ready. It sets a tone for the whole day in which you feel anxious and as if you're constantly racing to catch up.

Now think about a morning where you don't have to be anywhere in a hurry – perhaps a weekend, or a holiday. How different do you feel when your morning has been calm and leisurely instead of frantic? How does the rest of the day unfold when you've started it gently?

A morning ritual that works for you is one that helps you to tap into that gentler, calmer version of yourself.

Creating morning rituals allows space for intention and contemplation – let the start of your day be a reflection of the way you intend to move through the rest of it. It is so important to feel a sense of purpose for the day ahead.

Think about how to adapt these everyday rituals into ones that will allow you to feel your best.

CANDLELIT MORNING

This is a ritual for dark winter mornings, before the sun has risen. Rather than switching on electric lights as soon as you wake up, maintain the winter darkness for a little longer and reach for some candles instead.

Spend the first twenty minutes of your day in the warm glow of candlelight. You can sit quietly, or make a cup of tea, or just potter around the house. Feel how the candlelight allows you to transition slowly into your day.

We so often race from moment to moment, forgetting that transitions also deserve our attention and our respect. Taking time to honour this space between waking and the ever-present to-do list will set the tone for how you tackle the day ahead.

You might think this ritual is hard to practise if you live with other people, but we have a friend with children who wakes up ahead of her family especially to have this quiet candlelit time to herself.

As soon as the kids are up, the lights come on and her busy routine takes over, but she has had her moment to herself, and started the day peacefully.

COFFEEPOT MEDITATION

A friend of ours has one of those stovetop coffeepots that takes about ten minutes to percolate. She used to spend that time rushing around doing morning chores, trying not to waste the few minutes it took the coffee to be ready. Most mornings she ran out of the house wishing she'd had time to meditate, but not knowing where it would have fitted into her always-busy routine.

So she decided to change things and drop the chores, which she finally realised would always be there. Now she puts the coffee on the stove, then practises her meditation while waiting for it to boil. Linking meditation to her coffee habit helps fix it as part of her morning routine.

Make taking time for yourself part of your morning routine. Most of us pay attention to how we look before we leave the house, but we should also bring our awareness to how we feel before we face the world outside. We believe that a daily check-in with your headspace is as important as getting dressed or brushing your teeth.

You may not have a stovetop coffeepot, but is there a similar habit that you can link to a moment of morning stillness and contemplation?

Consciously find those spaces in which you can be still.

GET CREATIVE

You're probably already sick of hearing that it's not a great idea to sleep with your phone in your room, or to pick it up and start scrolling the moment you wake up. It can be hard to break this habit, so why not try to replace it with a small ritual instead?

Rather than picking up your phone first thing, pick up a notebook and a pen. Early morning is a time when we are full of imagination and creativity – especially in that place between sleep and being fully awake. You may remember your dreams really clearly in those waking moments.

Use this time to write or doodle for a few minutes. Put on paper your plans and hopes for the day. Tapping into your creativity helps you choose the tone of the day ahead of you, instead of having your phone dictate it to you with a barrage of news alerts.

Try not to get too hung up on getting the words exactly right, or making the drawing something impressive and beautiful. This isn't about being perfect, it's about letting your imagination flow without hesitation or judgement. You might be surprised by what emerges in these early morning pages.

WAKE ME UP BEFORE YOU GO-GO

Katia's most recent morning ritual came about because her youngest hates getting up, and Huxley's bad morning moods were hard on the whole family.

The alarm now goes off with Wham's 'Wake Me Up Before You Go-Go' and everyone has a little morning dance party in the bedroom. Huxley being in a good mood in the morning means one less hassle to deal with, which is a total win for any mum.

Huxley sees this new routine as fun, and doesn't necessarily recognise that he's feeling good because he's got his body moving first thing. But we know from experience (and science!) that getting your body moving is a guaranteed morning mood-lifter.

We can find ourselves believing that morning exercise means we should do an hour at the gym, or a full yoga routine, when actually a dance along to the radio might be all that you need.

Try to find time in the morning to move your body in some way. And if you can laugh while doing it, we think that's all the better.

A DAILY INTENTION

This is such a simple ritual, but one that has a transformative effect on your day. Make yourself a promise that you can't come back into your home today – or any day – until you've done something good for another person.

We first read about this ritual in an interview with actress Olivia Colman, and immediately adopted it ourselves as it's such a beautiful idea.

Don't feel that you have to make a huge grand gesture every day, or you'll be unlikely to keep it going. Keep it small and achievable. Perhaps help someone with their shopping bags, or give someone your seat on the train. In the winter it can be good to carry a few pairs of warm socks in your bag to offer to people living on the streets – it's hard to keep clean and dry when you have nowhere safe to sleep.

Although we think donating money to charity is a great thing to do, we've realised that an online payment, while super convenient, can distance us from the people who need our help by keeping them out of sight and out of mind. This small daily ritual helps to connect us to those around us, and in helping each other we all benefit.

Feel how this intention shifts your attention from your own concerns onto helping others. When you are looking out for opportunities to do something good, it's harder to feel bad about yourself (or anyone else).

MAKE THE BED

This is one of those tiny rituals that seems insignificant, yet has the power to transform how you feel about yourself. By making the bed in the morning, and tidying your bedroom before you leave the house, you are demonstrating self-respect and self-care. The act of looking after yourself and your environment will spill over into everything else you do.

If you think this seems too small a change to make a difference, try it before you dismiss it. US Admiral William McRaven gave a famous commencement speech in which he suggested that, if you want to change the world, you should start by making your bed, because the achievement of small tasks leads to the achievement of bigger ones.

We can fall into the trap of thinking that changing our lives comes from dramatic moves such as a new home or a new relationship, when it is often the smallest actions that make the biggest difference.

Instead of thinking of making your bed as a boring chore, remind yourself how good it feels to come home to a welcoming, restful bedroom every day. And if your day's been terrible, a made bed reminds you that your day is over and you can start afresh tomorrow.

SPRING

There is something about the transition from winter to spring that gives many of us the urge to shake things up and change them around.

The first bright day of spring sunshine can mean we suddenly see the dirty windows or the dusty shelves that we haven't noticed on dark winter evenings. We sense the days becoming lighter, and the energy shifting from a time of hibernation to a time of awakening and growth.

It's good to find ways to mark the change of season from dark to light, both in terms of bringing the brightness of spring into your home and by considering which parts of your life could do with a bit of fresh energy and focus.

SHAKE THE HOUSE!

One of our favourite rituals at this time of year is a good old spring clean. In Persian tradition, spring is the time for the *khaneh-tekani*, which literally means 'shaking the house'. It is said to stem from the Zoroastrian belief that cleanliness keeps evil away.

During the *khaneh-tekani*, the whole household joins in to scrub and clean every corner of the home. Rugs and curtains are washed, broken furniture is repaired or thrown out, and the space is cleared of all debris from the past.

The house is then filled with fragrant flowers, such as hyacinths, to refresh the air with the scent of spring.

What steps can you take to shake up your own house to rid it of the stagnant air of winter and welcome in the new season? Remind yourself why you're shaking the house, so your ritual has a sense of purpose instead of feeling like a housekeeping chore.

You can follow each of these steps in one day, or just use a few of the suggestions at a time. If you live with other people, bring in everyone to do their share, don't turn this into a massive to-do list just for you.

* Shake your curtains and rugs outdoors – just hang them out of a window if you don't have any outside space. If you can hang them on a washing line and hit them with a stick or an umbrella to get rid of dust, all the better (or get the kids to do it, they love this).

* Air duvets, cushions and pillows outside in the sunshine.

* If your furniture or crockery is broken or chipped, either repair it or throw it away. Ensure the objects you have around you are in good working order, and don't let your energy be depleted by constantly seeing things that need to be fixed.

* Some Iranians burn the herb wild rue to cleanse and fragrance their homes after the spring clean. This can be hard to find, so we like to use either sage or palo santo instead.

* Wash your floors with a few drops of a fresh and energising citrus essential oil added to the water. We love bergamot, wild orange or grapefruit.

* Get rid of clutter and only keep the things you really love. When we open up space in one part of our lives, we invite a sense of spaciousness everywhere.

* Open all the windows and let the fresh air bring in the new energy of spring.

* Fill your house with spring flowers. This doesn't have to cost a fortune – big bunches of daffodils or narcissi are really affordable at this time of year.

MAKE AN ALTAR

We know the word altar can make some people feel weird. Remember that an altar doesn't have to be religious, it's just a way to make a dedicated space in your home for the things that matter to you.

Think about when you go to someone's house and they have a table full of framed family photos. They may not think of their table as an altar, but it's a place that shows us, and them, the people and memories that are dear to their heart.

The change of seasons can be a great time to create an altar. For spring, you may want to think of items that represent new growth, manifestations and intentions.

* Find a place for your altar where you can easily see it every day. If you feel self-conscious, you can always set it up in a cupboard so it's hidden.

* Clear a surface of clutter so there is plenty of space for the objects you have chosen. You can use a piece of cloth as the base of your altar if you like.

* We write down our intentions, big and small, and add them to the altar, sometimes with photographs or images.

* We like to put a candle on our altar to represent light and hope. Lighting this daily reminds you of your intentions.

* We love to use crystals, depending on what we're trying to attract. Try rose quartz for love and sun pyrite for manifestation. Take a look at page 184 for suggestions about other crystals and their properties.

* Consider burning palo santo, a sage stick, or incense for cleansing.

RISE WITH THE SUN

Most of us only pause to watch the sunrise when we're on holiday somewhere beautiful, but the sun rises and sets every day no matter where you are. Even if you're not able to see the horizon from inside your home, you can still find a place where the sunlight can reach you.

For one week, try to rise with the sun each morning. This is easiest to practise in the early part of spring, before the sun rises super early.

Find out the sunrise times for the week you choose and set your alarm to wake you a few minutes earlier. Don't switch on any lights – or grab your phone – when you wake up. Instead, just notice what the light is like before the sun comes up.

Sit quietly and watch the light begin to come in. Notice how the room changes as the sun gets higher. Feel the light of the sun on your skin – even if there is no warmth in it, can you sense your body responding?

Take a moment to feel connected to the daily cycle of dark and light. Be grateful for all that the sun brings to us – warmth, light, the growth of plants, the entire ecosystem that supports us.

SCRUB AWAY THE WINTER

Spring is a time when we feel the urge to shed the heavy layers of winter clothing, and show a bit more of ourselves to the world. We might get a haircut or a pedicure so we're ready for the long-awaited sunshine. Even the birds change their colours at this time of year; it's part of the natural cycle.

In many traditions, before everyone had their own bathroom at home, the change of seasons was the time for people to gather together at the hammam or the bath house for a seasonal cleanse.

We love to use this salt scrub before showering, to feel like we're scrubbing away the old season and making ourselves fresh and clean for the new. It's like shedding your old skin.

If you have sensitive skin, you might want to make this scrub with sugar instead, as it's gentler. Use a maximum of ten drops of essential oil to 100g of salt.

SALT SCRUB

- 100g fine salt (we use pink Himalayan)
- 50g coconut oil, warmed gently until it is liquid
- 5 drops of geranium essential oil, for optimism
- 5 drops of lavender essential oil, for relaxation

Mix all of the ingredients together. Store any leftovers in a glass jar with a sealable lid.

A NEW BABY

New life is by far the biggest beginning of all – for the baby, the mum and the family. It can be an incredibly intense time, which makes it all the more important to find gentle and simple rituals that honour the enormous changes that the family is experiencing.

There are many traditional rituals around the birth of a baby, from baptism to baby naming ceremonies. We're guessing you probably already have an idea of the big rituals that you'd like to practise to formally welcome the baby. Our ideas are for some more intimate rituals that allow for moments of contemplation and connection, which we hope can help you prepare for and welcome the new arrival.

If you are a new mother, be gentle to yourself at this testing time. You might not be able to manage even the simplest rituals in those early weeks, and that's fine. Remember that a ritual is supposed to be there to support you, not to make you feel bad. We know that a mother's prayer for her baby is the most powerful of all intentions.

PREGNANCY RITUAL

This is an intimate, personal ritual for you to practise alone, or perhaps with your partner.

Get a haramaki wrap, which is a traditional Japanese belly wrap made of soft cotton, designed to keep the belly warm during and post pregnancy. These are available in many stores and online, but if you can't find one, just use a piece of silk or organic cotton. Whichever fabric you use should be soft, comfortable and made of a natural fibre.

Take a marker pen and write loving messages for your unborn baby all over the cloth, such as:

May you have a gentle entry into the world.

May you be happy and healthy.

We love you and can't wait to meet you.

Wrap your belly and your baby in your prayers and wishes. If you don't have a cloth, an even simpler ritual is to whisper your prayers and wishes to the baby while rubbing your belly with organic coconut oil.

MOTHER BLESSING

Call us sentimental, but we think the real blessing of a baby shower comes not from the gifts but from the gathering together of friends with all of their shared love and hopes for the new mother and baby.

We like to share this alternative mother blessing at the last full moon before a baby's due date; this is because the round, full moon has traditionally been associated with the fullness of a pregnant belly. But really you can practise this ritual at any time in a woman's pregnancy.

Gather together the close friends of the mother-to-be, and choose a lovely long piece of silk thread – red is considered lucky by the Chinese, but select whatever colour you think the mother would like best.

Let each person bring with them a small charm that can be tied to the thread to represent their hopes and wishes for the mother and baby.

The mother sits, holding the thread, while her friends take turns in bringing their charms to her to be threaded on. The meaning of each charm will be personal to the giver, and they can share with the mother why they have chosen it for her.

At the end of this mother blessing ritual, the mother-to-be has a long necklace filled with charms from those she loves. She can then wear or hold this necklace while in labour, and afterwards, to remind her of the support and love that surrounds her.

WELCOMING THE BABY

Take time to prepare and think of a message for you and your partner to whisper to your baby as the first words they hear when they come into the world. Choose your words carefully and think of them as a mantra that the baby can carry forward with them into their new life.

Imagine you were the baby coming into the world. What would you want the first words you hear to be?

Perhaps you want to wish good health for your baby, or strength. Perhaps you want to tell them of the people who are waiting to meet them and love them. Your wishes for your baby will be personal to you and your situation; take time to think of them.

You may want to write these words down to give to your child later, to show them how welcomed and loved they were from that very first day.

Be kind to yourself with this ritual; if you have had a difficult birth, you may not be able to say these things to your baby straight away. The thought and the intention alone is enough.

DAILY RITUALS FOR NEW MOTHERS

Any mother of a new baby will tell you there is a lot of repetition in those early months. The constant treadmill of breastfeeding, nappy changing and soothing a crying baby can be bloody exhausting.

It can sometimes help to bring a bit of gentle mindfulness to these repetitive daily tasks.

* When you're bathing your baby, you can send a little prayer for the happiness of your baby, and the happiness of all beings.

* When you're feeding your baby, instead of scrolling through your phone, bring your attention to your breath and count the inhalation to the count of two, and the exhalation to the count of four.

* When you're pacing with your baby on your shoulder, trying to get them to sleep, try counting your steps. This can stop your thoughts spiralling into those 'will I ever sleep again?' panics, especially in the middle of the night.

Don't beat yourself up if you can't manage this at first. Breastfeeding is hardly meditative if you're struggling with a baby that won't latch on. And we know bathtime can be super stressful and not at all the splashy playtime we might have hoped for.

Just allow yourself to be in the moment exactly as it is, and remember that – good or bad – this moment will pass.

MEETING THE NEWBORN

We think anyone visiting a family with a brand new baby should bring useful things, such as a home-cooked meal or a cake to share with visitors. And we know the best gifts to new mothers are often those you can't see, such as holding the baby so she can take a shower, changing the sheets on her bed, or taking her toddler to the park.

It can also be lovely to bring a small symbolic gift for the baby the first time you meet them. We like gifts that are creative and that represent a quality or intention for the baby to guide it through its life. It could be something as simple as an amethyst crystal, which is said to bring calmness, soothing and protection.

The parents can make a little shelf in the baby's room where all of his or her guiding charms are kept to protect and watch over them.

You can add to the charms and homemade gifts on each birthday. When Katia's son Jonah turned one, Nadia made him a little painting which she framed and he still has it on his wall ten years later.

A NEW HOME

A new home can represent so much – a fresh start, a growing family or a change of circumstances. Whatever the reason for moving, it's good to bring your most hopeful intentions to your new space. We have moved a lot in our lives, and rituals have helped us find a sense of coming home, wherever we are. We hope some of these will resonate with you.

CLEARING OUT OLD ENERGY

You wouldn't get into a bath in a new home without cleaning it first, so think of clearing your home as a kind of energetic cleaning that means you aren't sitting in someone else's bathwater.

This isn't about bad vibes, or exorcism, so let go of the creepy idea that your new home might have 'bad energy' – it's not that someone else's energy is bad, it's just not *yours*!

You can use this ritual even if you haven't moved house but you just want to clear the energy of an old roommate, a past relationship or maybe just a difficult home situation that you'd like to put behind you.

* Place small dishes of salt in the corners of each room. Leave for a few hours, or even a day, then throw away the salt. In feng shui, salt is believed to absorb negative energy and bring a space back to neutrality.

* Open all the windows, then burn a sage stick or incense to clear the air.

* Clap your hands loudly in each room to break up stagnant energy. Feng shui aims for the flow of energy in a space, so that nothing gets stuck.

INTRODUCING YOURSELF
TO YOUR HOME

When you arrive at your new home, take the opportunity to sit in it for a while, before you move anything in.

Find the middle of your house, the place that feels like the centre of the home. Sit in this place, take a few deep breaths and let your new home know you are here. You can even say hello out loud.

We know it sounds nuts, and maybe we are, but we have literally done this in every place we have lived.

The conversation sounds a bit like this:

'Hi, new home. We are here and we are really excited to live in you. Thank you for providing shelter and a safe place for us to live. We know not everyone is as lucky as we are, and we are very grateful for being given the opportunity to live here.'

Say anything else you may want to add to this little conversation. Take a few more deep breaths and just sit in the feeling of your new home. You can light a candle and take a moment to let the house welcome your energy in.

A NEW HOME BLESSING

This is a really beautiful ritual we love to do once we have moved everything in and the new home has taken form.

Buy some fresh flowers and pick the flower heads off the stems. Take a tea light and a small plate for each room, including the bathroom and the space by the front door. Place a tea light in the centre of each plate and arrange the flowers around it.

Place a plate in each room, light the candle and set a little prayer or intention for that particular space.

You can do this by meditating in each room or write the prayers down and place them in the room – be as creative as you want.

In the living room you might wish for family harmony, in a child's bedroom a feeling of safety and nurturing. In the bedroom you might wish for a loving and passionate relationship. In the bathroom we always wish for good elimination (it matters!).

Fill your new home with the intentions and wishes of everyone who will live there. Make sure you blow out all candles before you leave the house or go to bed.

LOVE THY NEIGHBOUR

Everyone loves a nice neighbour. Whether you're the new neighbour or the existing one, why not give a small gift that represents the relationship you hope to develop?

Creating harmonious neighbourhoods is a responsibility we all share. Don't wait for someone else to make the effort to say hello, or think it's not really a priority when you've only just moved in. We're not saying you have to be best friends with all of your neighbours, but a small gesture goes a long way, especially early on in a relationship.

The traditional Jewish housewarming gift is one of bread and salt, and sometimes honey. Bread and salt signify the necessities of life, and honey represents a wish that life will be sweet. The gift of food is also a way to show that you wish for your neighbour's pantry to always be full – both literally and metaphorically.

We like to bake a cake or cookies to demonstrate the sweetness and harmony that good neighbours show each other. If you can't bake, just buy something – it's all about the intention.

A NEW YEAR

It's quite comforting to know there are several New Year's Days in the calendar. There's January 1st, Chinese New Year, Jewish New Year and several others, and each one feels like a chance to start again.

We grew up in Hong Kong and our mum still visits the temple every Chinese New Year to buy us a little charm to bring us good luck for the year. She would like us to wear these in our bras, so they're literally close to us at all times, but we just keep them in our wallets!

Let your New Year rituals, whenever you celebrate them, represent the qualities you want to bring with you into the year ahead.

NEW YEAR INTENTIONS

Take a quiet moment at New Year to reflect on three things you'd like to let go of from the old year. Write these down, and try to be specific and clear.

I am ready to let go of what no longer serves me.

I am ready to let go of trying to control everything.

I am ready to let go of not accepting myself as I am.

Then reflect on three things you'd like to welcome in the New Year. Make these intentions positive, instead of punishing.

I am kind to myself and others.

I am present in my relationships.

I love my body and all that it does for me.

If you've made an altar, you can leave your intentions there so you can return to them throughout the year.

A NEW YEAR CLEAN

There are lots of traditions around the Chinese New Year that we still celebrate, and use for the Western New Year, too. One of these rituals is a big clean of the house in preparation for the coming year.

In Chinese the word 'dust' sounds the same as the word 'old', so it's doubly important to make sure the home is as clean as possible. You want to be sure that the old year is fully cleared out before the new year begins.

Wash the floors and the walls, pushing all the dust and dirt of the old year towards the front door, and out of the house.

Change the sheets, tidy everything away and imagine the New Year as a guest that you're welcoming into your fresh and clean home.

It's traditional to do the big clean on New Year's Eve because it's believed that giving the house a clean on New Year's Day washes away your luck for the coming year, so make sure the massive New Year's Eve party happens at the house of someone who doesn't believe in this kind of stuff!

MAKE A NOISE

In Chinese tradition firecrackers are set off at New Year to disperse the old stagnant energy and make space for the new.

If you can't make it to a fireworks celebration, set off party poppers, bang some pan lids together or just clap loudly around the house.

Think about the new energy that you will bring in to replace the old.

TOAST YOUR WISHES

We find most people are really happy to get on board with a ritual that involves champagne! If you don't drink alcohol, you can do this with anything else you like, such as a sparkling elderflower drink. We picked up this ritual from Russian friends who love a party.

You will need a bottle of champagne, glasses and a packet of cigarette papers, or any other paper that burns quickly.

This ritual is practised in the last few seconds of the old year, as the countdown to midnight begins.

* Pour everyone a glass of champagne.

* Have each person write down their wish for the new year on a piece of cigarette paper.

* Take a match and light the paper. Hold it over the champagne glass and let it burn so that the ashes fall into the drink.

* Everyone then drinks their champagne (and their wish), as the new year begins.

PAUSE and think about what you would like to begin on this day, this month, this year.

PAY ATTENTION to how you feel when you contemplate new beginnings, big and small. Do you feel excited? Nervous? Where in your body do you feel those sensations?

SET YOUR INTENTION What is the goal or the dream that you would like to begin? And what ritual could you start today that will support you, and make space for your new beginnings?

inviting

'We are what we think. All that we are arises with our thoughts. With our thoughts, we make the world.' *Buddha*

One of our favourite writers, Anne Lamott, says the only three prayers anyone needs are 'help', 'thanks' and 'wow'. We like to think of this as the help section of the book. It's okay to ask for a little help in certain areas of your life – no one has it all together all the time.

Inviting and asking for what we want can make us feel vulnerable and sometimes even fearful, but it's in that vulnerability that we can really grow. It is pretty brave to allow yourself to think about what might be missing in your life, and to ask for it. Being clear about your needs, whether that's with yourself or with others, can be a very powerful force for change.

If it's a romantic relationship you want to invite, think about the qualities you would like the other person to have – kind, funny, caring? Think about how you would like to feel in that relationship – safe, loved, adored?

If you're asking for abundance, think about how that might manifest itself in your life – would you be more generous, more able to give to others in need? Is your desire for abundance really about security and safety?

Don't get too hung up on the details of what you're inviting in, because what you ask for may not come in the exact package you imagined. We have to be open and curious about how our wishes might arrive, and we have to be ready to receive them.

All rituals are a kind of invitation. Here are some we hope you'll try.

INVITING LOVE

Now we don't believe in casting magic spells for love, but we do believe in being clear about what you want to invite. Remember, the results may not be immediate – it's unlikely there's going to be a knock on the door the moment you finish your ritual – but paying attention to your needs will help you think more deeply about what new love might look like.

THE LOVE CORNER

According to feng shui, you can find the love corner of your house by standing at the front door of your home, facing inside. From this point locate the far right corner of your home – that's your love corner. If you live in a flat, use the front door to your flat, rather than the one to the whole building.

ADD

Symbols of love – these will be unique to you, but objects that are red, white or pink are associated with love.

Photographs of happy couples.

Pairs of objects, such as two candles or tea lights.

Fresh flowers or a plant.

Two rose quartz crystals – this is the crystal most associated with love.

GET RID OF

Pictures of exes or photos of just one person.

Prickly and spiky plants.

Games and toys (you don't want to be inviting players!).

Television or other distractions.

Baggage (literally – no suitcases).

No rubbish bin.

LOVE YOUR BEDROOM

When it comes to love, the bedroom is a space that needs some real consideration. It should be a place that feels safe and inviting, even if you're the only one sleeping there. Your environment tells you, and everyone else, a lot about how you feel about yourself. Whether you're in a relationship or not, make that message loving and welcoming.

This ritual uses a little feng shui and a little space clearing to create a room that is open to a loving relationship.

* Add balance to your bedroom – that means two bedside tables, two bedside lights, equal numbers of pillows. The space should be welcoming to a partner, rather than being set up for just one person.

* Get rid of furniture that is broken or damaged.

* Avoid mirrors that face your bed – this is said to deplete the energy of the sleeper, and also to invite the negative energy of third parties into a romantic relationship.

* Avoid too many photographs in the bedroom, especially of kids and parents, so you don't feel watched!

* Try not to use the space under your bed for storage – you want the energy to flow around the bedroom. If you have to keep things under the bed, make sure they're organised, and kept clean.

* Clear a drawer, or space in your wardrobe – literally make space for someone new.

* Think about making space in your life for a new relationship, too – do you like to fill every minute with activity? Where would a new person fit into your life?

A DATE NIGHT RITUAL

This is a ritual that we like to practise before going on a date, whether that's with someone new or a long-term partner. When we have taken time to take care of ourselves, and to feel the best version of ourselves, we feel as if we're so much more fun to hang out with.

Run a bath and add a handful of dead sea salts for cleansing, a tablespoon of coconut oil for moisturising, and five to ten drops of essential oils. We recommend these oils before a date (or turn to page 180 for a guide to other essential oils and their benefits):

Rose
Associated with love, and said to boost self-esteem and confidence.

Jasmine
Uplifting and energy-boosting.

Ylang ylang
Calming, relaxing, and also said to act as an aphrodisiac . . .

Light tea lights or candles around the bath and switch off other lights. Maybe play some music that gets you in the mood – keep it fun and uplifting, no sad songs, please!

Sit in your bath and really take the time to think about the kind of date you'd like to have tonight. Even if it's a first date that you're not sure about, still make the effort. Remember, this ritual is more for you than for the other person.

Invite love in whatever form it might arrive.

LOVE FOR ALL BEINGS

Often when we talk about love we think of romantic love, or love between individuals, rather than love for all beings. But there is love all around us if we can stay open to it. And the best way to stay open is to look for ways to be loving in our day-to-day lives.

There is a saying, sometimes attributed to Gandhi, that we should be the change we wish to see in the world. In times when we feel the world around us is harsh and unkind, that is when our compassion and love is needed most of all. Let the change start with you through one of these simple daily rituals.

* Choose a day in your week where you make a conscious effort to spark a happy conversation with strangers. Compliment someone's outfit, or their smile. Ask them about the book they're reading. It might feel weird at first but you will soon relax into it and you might even have fun.

* Take a 'good news' day, where you don't listen to the news, or the radio, or catch up on social media. Feel how much more positive your mood is after a day off from the never-ending news cycle, and notice how your interactions with others are more pleasant.

* Keep change in your pockets so it's easy to give to people in need, and harder to make the excuse that you don't have time to stop. If you can't afford to give money, you can still stop to say hello and ask someone how they're doing today.

* Spend a day trying to love and appreciate everyone you encounter. This one is bloody hard, especially if you live in a big and crowded city, but it is a great practice. When someone shoves in front of you, let go of your annoyance and think, 'I'm sorry you're clearly having a crappy day; feel better.'

WRITE YOURSELF A LOVE LETTER

We find it so easy to write a letter to someone we love and tell them all the great things we feel about them, but what about writing those things about yourself?

Don't just scribble this note down on a Post-it. Imagine that you are sending a letter to someone you love – make the effort by using lovely stationery or a beautiful notebook.

Light a candle and take a few deep breaths (this ain't going to be easy for some of us).

What do you like about yourself? What is your best quality? What do your friends love about you? What are you really great at – show off to yourself. What makes you proud of yourself?

When we wrote these letters to ourselves it was really challenging. It felt so cheesy and embarrassing at first, but it was actually a pretty incredible exercise. We'd still be totally mortified if anyone saw the letters we wrote, but when we read them back we felt pretty good about ourselves.

Keep your love letter somewhere safe. Then, when you're having a difficult time, take it out and re-read it to remind yourself that you're doing just fine.

ACCEPT YOUR FLAWS

Now this one's a bit trickier. Write a letter to the things you don't like about yourself. Make it a kind and loving letter that accepts the flaws we all have. When we did this ritual we had no problem finding our own flaws, but we definitely found it hard being loving towards them.

If that sounds like you, imagine you are writing this letter to a child you really love. When a toddler has a massive tantrum we don't tell them they're a terrible, damaged, awful person. We try to understand why they might be behaving that way. Offer yourself the same kind of understanding.

'I accept my crazy temper and how I can fly off the handle sometimes. I'd like to be more patient, and I am working on this, but I also know intensity is part of my character. Being passionate about things can be a strength of mine. I ask for the wisdom to know the difference between being passionate and totally losing it.'

A clever therapist once told us that accepting your flaws is like knowing and loving the underwear you have on. So if someone says to you, 'I can see your knickers', your response isn't embarrassment and shame but, 'Thanks for noticing. I love this pair.'

INVITING
ABUNDANCE

The best way we know to invite abundance into our lives is to be grateful for the abundance we already have. When we focus on what we don't have, we live in lack, and that is the opposite of living an abundant life. When you appreciate that your life is full of things to be grateful for, you will find you already feel rich.

If you're really struggling to feel grateful, start small – be glad for your health, the food on your plate, the roof over your head. Those simple things that we fortunate people take for granted may be someone else's dream of abundance right now.

There are people with a lot of material possessions who still focus on what they don't have, and others who have little but are so very abundant in their attitude. Make a decision about who you want to be.

GRATITUDE

The simplest way to bring gratitude into your daily life is to focus on the food you eat. It is a position of real privilege to be able to take your regular mealtimes for granted, and even sometimes to think of them as something tedious, 'Oh god, not pasta again'.

* Before each meal, take a moment to think about how grateful you are for this food. You don't have to close your eyes or put your hands into prayer, just look at your food and silently say a simple 'thank you' in your head. This one takes a bit of discipline to practise daily, but once you get into it, it's a great little ritual.

* If you have more time or want to close your eyes and take a few moments, you can think not just about the food, but also the chain of the people who sold it to you, the delivery drivers, the farmers, the sun, the earth and the water. Feel the thread that connects you to the very beginning of a seed planted so that you could have food to eat. We love to practise this ritual with other people – perhaps you could do it with your family – to create an awareness of the cycle of life and ourselves within it.

GIVING TO OTHERS

We were taught by our first yoga teacher, Gurkmukh, that when you do something for someone it comes back to you multiplied by seven. Not that we think this is the only reason to be generous, but it's an encouraging thought.

There is a famous saying that we make a living by what we get, but we make a life by what we give. When it feels like we are lacking, we hoard the things that belong to us instead of sharing them. Let your feeling of abundance allow you to give to others, knowing that you are also giving to yourself.

Invite consciousness and awareness into your day to find opportunities to be generous.

Give an unexpected gift to someone you love. Don't wait for a birthday or for Christmas. Really take time to think about the person's likes so that your gift is personal; nothing is more rewarding than a gift that says you have been seen and understood.

Make something for someone. If you can't afford to buy something, you can make them a painting or a poem or even just a card. The love and thought that comes with a homemade gift is so much more meaningful than an expensive present given with no thought behind it.

Give your time to someone who you know needs it. One of our friends made a book of homemade 'Auntie's babysitting vouchers', so that her stressed-out sister wouldn't feel embarrassed to ask for the help she really needed.

THE ART OF RECEIVING GENEROUSLY

Inviting is only one part of manifesting your desires – you have to be ready to receive, too. This can be the hardest part. Sometimes we only see afterwards that we turned away the very thing we wanted because we didn't recognise it at the time.

When receiving feels hard, it often comes from a place of not feeling worthy of the gift. Or it is related to a judgement that you have around receiving – do you think accepting the generosity of others makes you needy? Or an imposition?

Remember that when you don't receive you are not allowing the giver the enjoyment of giving.

We like the metaphor of moonlight, which comes to us on Earth from the moon receiving and reflecting the light of the sun. When you are able to receive, you and the giver both share in the light.

Shine on.

HEART OPENING RITUAL

In yoga, the front of the heart, on your chest, is associated with giving. The back of your heart, your back ribs, is associated with receiving. Ideally both are balanced, so we can give and receive equally.

In modern life we spend so much time hunched over laptops and mobile phones that we close off our front heart and harden the back of our heart. Let this ritual bring you back into balance.

* Find a comfortable seated position somewhere calm and quiet.

* Rub one drop of sandalwood essential oil between the palms of your hands, then rub it on to your chest in a clockwise direction, like you're making a spiral. Sandalwood oil is supposed to connect the mind and the heart, and bring you to your highest self.

* Extend your arms out in front of you, palms touching. On an inhale, open your arms as wide as you can, lifting your heart centre so that your chest rises and your chin slightly lifts. As you exhale, bring your palms back to the starting position, rounding your back gently. Continue inhaling and exhaling like this for a full minute.

MANIFESTING

There are a lot of rituals out there for manifesting, or bringing a desire into existence. We like to think of manifesting as opening ourselves up to the abundance that is already out there, rather than coming to the rituals from a place of feeling as if we are lacking in some way.

It's important that we don't see manifesting simply as a shopping list, not least because we'll only be disappointed when the universe doesn't work like a magical Santa to deliver everything we've asked for. Stay open, stay receptive and stay aware of the blessings that come when you least expect them.

Approach manifestation with positivity and optimism, and we hope your dreams come true.

A RITUAL AHEAD OF A JOB INTERVIEW

Interviews can be totally nerve-wracking. A lot of what makes us nervous is the fear of the unknown, and being caught out and exposed as unworthy and undeserving. We like to practise this very simple ritual before any big interview, to settle our nerves and leave us feeling confident.

* The night before the interview, light a candle to focus your attention and write down how you see your new job, how you want to feel in it, what you would like to achieve and how you want to be respected and seen in that role. If writing isn't your thing, make a collage of pictures instead, so you can really visualise yourself in the new job.

* Place your visualisations, written or illustrated, somewhere safe. For us, this is usually on a small altar. We like to put visualisations under a piece of black tourmaline, which is said to be an excellent stone for eliminating negative thoughts, anxieties and feelings of unworthiness.

* On the day of the interview, put a tiger's eye stone in your pocket or your bag. Tiger's eye is great for staying grounded, centred and courageous. It keeps your mind clear and logical and helps you in difficult situations. Even if you don't believe in this kind of thing, having a little lucky charm with you will make you feel better.

And finally, trust that what is meant to be, will be. If you don't get the job, it doesn't mean that there's anything wrong with you. It just means the right job is yet to come.

AN ALTAR FOR MANIFESTING

When we wrote our first book, we put a lot of effort into imagining its success as clearly and in as much detail as possible. Katia wrote down all her hopes and wishes in a copy of the actual book once it was printed, then put crystals all over it to magnify her dreams. Nadia built a book altar in her flat, and it's still up today.

It's important to recognise that as well as doing the manifesting, we did the work! We didn't just do some rituals for success then sit back and wait for the universe to send us what we'd asked for. When it comes to manifesting your desires, remember that you will have to put the work in too.

Creating a manifesting altar is really simple:

* Find a clear, clean space.

* Have at least one candle on your altar – and light it daily to bring your attention back to your manifesting intentions.

* Add objects and pictures that mean something to you – in our case we put a photo of our dad, because we like to feel he's watching over us.

* When it comes to crystals we used sun pyrite, because that is the mineral of manifestation. We also had quartz crystals for clarity, and carnelian, which is a stone for taking big actions. So our bases were really covered. Have a look at page 184 for more details on crystals.

You may think crystals are a bit pointless, and that's fine too. The altar is about what matters to you, and just as everyone's dreams are different, so are everyone's altars.

BE A VISION HOLDER

Sometimes our wishes for others can be stronger than our wishes for ourselves. This can be particularly true if you're a parent. We don't believe it's possible to manifest outcomes for someone else – you always have to do the work for yourself. But we do believe that you can be a support for someone else's manifestation.

We love the term 'vision holder' for someone who is able to hold on to a beautiful vision for a person who may not be able to hold it for themselves.

Perhaps your friend is sick, or your kid is being bullied at school, or someone you love is grieving. When they can't see a way out of their situation, light the way for them with your love and intention. You don't have to tell them that you're acting as their vision holder – in fact, it's probably best not to; it's about them, not you.

In some Native American traditions, the vision is said to be held in an object, such as a charm or a stone, and worn in a pouch around the neck. You can do this for yourself, but we like it best as a beautiful gift for someone else.

* Make a really, really simple altar – one that would be barely recognisable as an altar to most people. Just put up a picture of your person and add fresh flowers and a candle.

* Light the candle each morning and evening, and take that time to send them your wishes for safety, health and happiness.

* If you want to add a little more, write down your prayers for the other person (preferably on the back of a photograph of them) and either place it on your altar or sleep with it under your pillow.

* Buy a crystal or a small object or charm that has meaning to your person. Hold the crystal or the charm, and think of your person as happy and healthy. Then give it to them with all your good intentions and healing vibrations. This is especially good if you know someone who needs to go to chemo or other medical treatments regularly, so they can take your crystal in with them and hold it when they are feeling scared.

Respect the boundaries of the person for whom you're holding the vision. They may not want your opinion or even the burden of your attention if this is a really hard time for them. Allow your behaviour to be guided by what they need, rather than what you want for them.

PAUSE and consider what you want to invite into your life. This will change over time, so be sure to ask yourself this question regularly.

PAY ATTENTION to how you feel when you imagine receiving the things you wish for. Are you ready to receive and be grateful for them? If not, how can you make yourself ready?

SET YOUR INTENTION and be as clear and as specific as you can. Your intention should feel as real to you as if it has already happened.

changing

'Why do you want to shut out of your life any uneasiness, any miseries, or any depressions? For after all, you do not know what work these conditions are doing inside you.' *Rainer Maria Rilke*

Change is an interesting subject. We long for it and we fear it all at once. We say we want to change our lives, but when changes happen we often panic and fear that we're not ready. Some of us handle change with ease and elegance while others hang on to the status quo for dear life.

The only constant is that life changes whether we like it or not. It helps if we can remind ourselves that it is our resistance to change that causes us pain, not change itself. Rituals grant us the space to accept changes, both welcome and unwelcome. We can learn to see, as the Sufi mystic Rumi says, that unwanted changes may be preparing us for new delights that aren't yet clear to us.

We change, situations change, other people change, and there is not one damn thing we can do about it. All that is within our power is to try to traverse the terrain of change with as much grace as possible. Sometimes we see the giant wave coming, sometimes it takes us by surprise – we hope these rituals will help you get back up on the surfboard.

RITES OF PASSAGE

Every culture around the world has traditions and ceremonies that recognise the changes that all humans experience from birth to death. Rituals help us to mark the ways in which we develop as we grow up and grow older. These rituals don't have to be as big as the traditional bar or bat mitzvah, or as complex as some of the initiation ceremonies practised in tribal cultures, but we believe we should still mark rites of passage in ways that are meaningful.

We're all growing and learning every day, and it's rare for us to stop and acknowledge that. Let these rituals give you a moment to see how far you've come.

A BIRTHDAY JOURNAL

When you're young your birthday feels like the most exciting day of the year, what with the cake, the party and all of the presents. When you're older it can bring a mixture of feelings, and a sense of questioning ourselves about where you are and where you're going.

Once we're past twenty-one we tend to only celebrate the birthdays with a zero on the end, but we think every year is a kind of rite of passage that should be marked, whatever age you're at.

Birthdays are literally a celebration of being here on this earth, as the individual you are meant to be. There is nothing quite so special as the day you were born, so don't get down on it! You just made another orbit around the sun in one piece, and that is cause for celebration.

Think about how you have changed this year. How are you different to where you were this time last year? What passage have you been through? If you're unsure of this, maybe ask someone close to you – sometimes others can see these things more clearly!

A few days before your birthday, start to gather pictures of significant times from over the past year. We tend to store photos on our phones and computers but for this ritual you will need to actually print out the photos that have the most meaning for you.

Buy a journal or notebook that you are going to keep for birthdays only. After a few years your birthday journal will become a way for you to check in on how your feelings and goals change over time, and how you change, too.

On the day of your birthday, take out your journal and get ready to make a record of the year that has just passed.

* Write down three things that you found challenging this year and how you managed them.

* Now think about noticing things you did well this year; what made you proud of yourself?

* Write down three goals you have for the year ahead, big or small. Then add how you're going to achieve them – break them down into steps that feel achievable.

* Stick in the pictures and photographs that evoke a feeling or a memory of the past year.

Make your journal a personal reflection you can return to year after year.

ADOLESCENCE

Every culture has a rite of passage around the teenage years. In the Jewish tradition it's the bar or bat mitzvah at thirteen, while in Mexico a girl has her *quinceañera* at fifteen, and sweet sixteen parties are a big deal in America.

Traditionally, men's rites of passage can be quite barbaric, and to do with enduring painful trials – not something Katia wants to inflict on her sons!

We like to mark the passage of adolescence with this lovely ritual that isn't too embarrassing (even though we know that teenagers think *everything* is embarrassing). You can keep it to a few people, or, if your teenager agrees, turn it into a bigger celebration and have everyone gather together.

Around the time that a child turns thirteen, ask your closest friends and family to write a card or letter to them. This could be a piece of wisdom that has been passed down through the family or a wish for them as they grow into adulthood. It could be a gift, if you like, but ask people to keep these small and meaningful, they don't have to be fancy or expensive.

Either get a box that you can decorate or a blank notebook, and fill them with all that you have gathered from the people in your close circle.

You'll know best how to give the box or book to your teenager. Some kids would die of shame to receive this in front of others, so just present it to them at bedtime as a quiet acknowledgement of their movement from one stage of life to another. Others might be happy for the celebration to be more public.

Just because a teenager may find this ritual super mortifying doesn't mean they won't appreciate it. It's a way of showing them they have a tribe behind them to hold them up when they are going through such big changes.

SECOND SPRING RITUAL

Menopause is looked at with so much negativity in our culture, and spoken of (if at all) as something shameful and sad. But in Asian cultures, the menopause is called the 'second spring', in which a woman is liberated from the child-rearing years and comes into a time of sexual freedom and wisdom.

The menopause is considered to have happened a year from the day of your last ever period. You may have forgotten when that was, so we suggest you pick a date for this ritual when you feel you need a bit of help from the women who've gone before you.

Gather together your favourite women, and be sure to invite some older women whose advice and experience you value. If you're close to your mum, her experience will be really valuable here.

Sit in a circle and pour everyone a glass of red wine, or cherry juice if you don't drink. Light some candles and get ready for everyone to share their wisdom.

Ask everyone these three questions:

Who was I?

What have I learned?

Who am I now?

Allow each woman in turn to say something about what this new stage in life means to her. For some there may be tears, but hopefully there will be a whole lot of laughs too.

THE GIFT OF AGEING

We're used to seeing all kinds of beauty rituals on social media, with serums, moisturisers and fancy ingredients. Many of these beauty rituals come from a place of addressing your face as a problem, such as getting rid of fine lines or making yourself look younger. It's easy to find fault with your face, but try to look at it differently. See if you can start to look at yourself in the way that someone who loves you does.

Ageing is a privilege that not everyone gets to experience. The lines on your face tell the stories of your life, so learn to love them, and be grateful for the experiences the years have given you.

We like to take the time to massage in a face oil at night, and to really appreciate the skin we have, without wishing it was different. You can buy face oils, but a lot of them are really expensive, so here is one that we like to make ourselves.

FACE OIL

- 1 tbsp jojoba oil – which absorbs well into the skin
- ½ tbsp rosehip oil – which is moisturising
- ½ tbsp vitamin E – which is hydrating
- 5 drops of frankincense essential oil – an astringent that tones the skin
- 5 drops of geranium essential oil – an uplifting oil, great for hormonal balance
- A small glass bottle with a lid

Mix all the oils together and store in a glass bottle, away from direct sunlight.

Apply a few drops of the oil to your hands and massage it into your skin. We love the Louise Hay affirmation of looking yourself in the eye in the mirror and telling yourself, 'I love you, I really love you.' At first negativity will flow in and you'll feel ridiculous, but stick with it. Try to see – and love – the ageless part of yourself.

MOON RITUALS

The moon is in a constant process of change. Never still, it moves from darkness to light and back to dark again. Checking in with the lunar cycle reminds us that, just like the moon, we're not always going to be full and bright and shining. Sometimes we're going to be quiet and a little understated. The key is understanding that where we are right now isn't permanent, it's just a moment on the never-ending cycle of change.

The beauty of moon rituals is that they give us time each month to recalibrate our hopes and desires.

We've given a basic lunar ritual under the new moon heading, and offered adaptations for the other phases of the lunar cycle.

NEW MOON

A new moon, also called the dark moon, is traditionally considered the phase of greatest potential. At this time in the lunar cycle the moon is invisible in the sky. It's empty and receptive, ready for the planting of new seeds.

Set up a space for your altar or shrine. A good crystal for the new moon is labradorite, known as the crystal for transformation and new beginnings.

Light some candles and burn a sage stick around the altar and around yourself. Think of the sage as cleansing away your doubts and concerns about what you may or may not deserve.

Take a few deep breaths and on a piece of paper write down your thanks for the gifts you most wish to receive. Really imagine yourself actually receiving these gifts. When it comes to this ritual, we don't really mean wishing for material things like a new car or a lot of money, it's more the feeling of abundance that we're trying to connect to.

Thank you for the freedom that abundance brings me.

Thank you for the stability and safety I will feel in my new home.

Thank you for the fulfilment I will feel in my new job.

Place the paper on your altar, then sit for a few minutes, to feel like your dreams have settled.

WAXING MOON

This phase is when the moon is growing fuller, and is considered the best time for visualisation and creativity. We take the seeds we've planted in the new moon phase, and work to nourish and grow them during the waxing moon.

Set up and sage your altar, as above. Think about cleansing yourself of doubts about your creativity and worthiness.

The crystal we like to use for the waxing moon is carnelian, for courage and motivation.

Sit at your altar and invite inspiration to come to you. Ask for the awareness to recognise opportunities when they arrive – the waxing moon is seen as a time of collaboration and teamwork, so you're going to want to welcome those helpful partners when they come your way.

FULL MOON

This is said to be the time of the highest energy – lots of people find they can't sleep under a full moon. Hospital admissions go up, and more babies are born. The full moon is also said to be the time at which your new moon intentions come to fruition.

Sage yourself and your altar space. If you want to add a crystal, sun stone is good for this phase of the moon. It dispels fear and doubt and is a stone of abundance and prosperity.

Sit at the altar and look back at the intentions you set at the new moon. Pay attention to the way in which your wishes might have come true – it might not have been in the manner in which you hoped or expected. Give thanks for the gifts that have come your way.

The full moon is also considered to be a good time to get all your crystals (if you have them) and charge them under the light of the full moon to clear their energy. Just place them in your garden or on a windowsill for a few nights.

Our friend's mum taught us about moon bathing, and we love this ritual. When the moon is full, get yourself out and bathe in the moonlight for a few minutes. It's cooling and calming to the nervous system – the opposite of sunbathing.

WANING MOON

The waning moon is the phase in which the moon becomes less full, as it returns to the new moon state. It's a phase of reflection, release and letting go.

It's a good moment to consider letting go of addictions, bad relationships and anything that you feel is toxic in your life. We can slow down and make space for new behaviour in the new moon.

Sage yourself and your altar, and think about what you need to let go of at this waning moon.

For this phase of the moon we like a malachite on our altar for protection from negative energy.

Take several small pieces of paper and a ceramic or metal bowl (not plastic). Write down the things that you want to release at this time. Light a candle on your altar.

One by one, set light to the papers (over the bowl, so you don't set fire to anything else) and allow the flame to burn away the bad stuff.

CELEBRATING THE SEASONS

Just like the cycles of the moon, the changing of the seasons gives us another opportunity to tune into the natural world. In all cultures there are rituals and ceremonies that celebrate the qualities of the seasons, and the moments when they peak or change.

We use rituals around the seasons to establish the clear end of one stage and the beginning of another, and to reflect on our own endings and beginnings.

SPRING AND AUTUMN EQUINOX RITUALS

The equinox is a day of equilibrium, when the darkness of night and the light of day are of exactly equal length. From the spring equinox onwards, the days will be growing longer, lighter and hopefully warmer as we head into summer. After the autumn equinox, the days shorten as winter approaches.

The spring equinox falls towards the end of March, and the autumn equinox around the end of September. The exact date moves around from year to year, so you'll need to check online to be sure of the date for your ritual.

Equinoxes are a great time to think about equilibrium in your own life. How balanced are you feeling right now? What steps can you take to bring more balance to the way you live and work?

We like to gather our friends at each equinox to perform a little ritual together. It is good to feel that your friends support your hopes, and that you can offer support for theirs too.

* Prepare an altar, or perhaps just a table if you prefer.

* Light a candle on the altar or table.

* Sit together in a circle and write down your dreams for the six months ahead. Spring is the time to be thinking of planting seeds – new beginnings and possibilities. In autumn we focus on harvesting, abundance and what will sustain us through the winter.

* Share your intentions with the group (you may want to keep yours private, and that's fine too), then have everyone place their intentions on the altar.

* You can place a crystal on top of the intentions. We love sun pyrite for manifestation, fluorite for mental clarity and taking action, and pink tourmaline for joy, happiness and relaxation.

* Leave the intentions in place as long as you can (it's good if you can return to your spring intentions at the autumn equinox, and vice versa).

* Take a moment of silence together to reflect on the possibilities and potential of the coming season.

SOLSTICE RITUALS

Solstices are essentially the opposite to equinoxes. Instead of being about balance and equalibrium, they are about extremes. The winter solstice is when the day is shortest and the night longest, while the summer solstice is celebrated on the longest day of the year. Each represents the peak of a season, and of the year as a whole.

Traditionally the summer solstice is a time of great energy and celebration. The days are long, the sun is (hopefully) shining, and harvest is coming. Pagan cultures celebrated the sun god at the summer solstice, believing that as the sun was strongest on this day, the god was too.

The winter solstice is both a recognition of the darkest, most inward-looking night of the year, and a welcoming of the lengthening days that will follow.

The summer solstice is towards the end of June and the winter solstice is at the end of December – like equinoxes, these move around by a few days, so check online first before you plan your ritual. If you're in the southern hemisphere, these dates are the opposite way round, of course.

SUMMER SOLSTICE

Summer solstice celebrations are about enjoying the abundance that is brought to us by the sun. Traditionally this solstice is celebrated with outdoor gatherings of plenty of people, music and dancing. We definitely recommend having as many parties as you can manage while the sun shines late.

In ancient midsummer rites, fire was often used to represent the sun. Some Nordic traditions saw burning torches carried through the community, while in England hay bales were set alight in the fields in the belief that the fires would celebrate and strengthen the power of the sun.

For us, the summer solstice should be spent outside, if possible with your friends and a big bonfire. If a bonfire's out of the question, can you light a barbecue or a fire pit? You want something a bit more impressive and celebratory than just a candle, so that your friends can gather around it.

We love making flower crowns for people to wear at the celebration. They don't need to be complicated or exotic – a simple daisy chain will do – but they are a visual reminder of the bounty and the beauty of summer.

Ask everyone to bring a dish to share, especially those that use seasonal foods.

In ancient European traditions, herbs were believed to be at their most medicinally powerful at midsummer, and were harvested on this day. To honour this tradition, we like to use some herbs in our dishes, and also use them as an offering on our solstice bonfire. The traditional herbs used in these rites are summer plants such as chamomile, lavender, fennel, mint and meadowsweet.

Gather your friends around the fire and invite people to give thanks, out loud, for the things they are the most grateful for. Afterwards, everyone throws handfuls of herbs on the fire, then dances until the sun goes down.

WINTER SOLSTICE

Midwinter is traditionally a reflective, inward time of year. But it's also a season when we find ourselves rushing around between festive shopping and holiday parties.

We like to take the winter solstice as a time to retreat from some of the more hectic holiday season activities, and allow ourselves to sink into a moment of reflection and renewal.

Although it is the night of the longest darkness, the winter solstice has also traditionally been a celebration of the light that is returning to us from this point onwards in the year. In different cultures that might mean lighting a yule log or a menorah.

In keeping with the contemplation of the season, we'd suggest you keep your winter solstice ritual domestic and intimate. It's a great one to do alone or, if you'd like to share it, just invite a few close friends.

You will need one big pillar candle and as many small candles, or tea lights, as you can find. There should be at least one tea light per person.

* Place the pillar candle in the centre of your altar or table. This is your sun candle, which represents the return of the light. Make sure the room is dark, and light only the pillar candle.

* Either with your friends, or to yourself, thank the deep darkness of winter for its restoration and reflection.

* Slowly take each tea light in turn and light it from the sun candle. Place the lit tea lights around the pillar candle in a circle.

* When all the candles are lit, sit and contemplate what the return of the light means to you.

WHEN THE SHIT
HITS THE FAN

Let's be honest, not all change is great. Sometimes change feels terrible, especially when it comes out of nowhere and is not what you wanted.

At these times there's often not a lot you can do other than get through each day as best you can. Healthy routines will stabilise you in difficult times; keeping to regular bedtimes and making time for nourishing meals will support you as you try to get back on your feet.

Rituals can help, too, by giving you a moment of contemplation in the eye of the storm.

GROUNDING RITUAL

In the midst of change, especially unwanted change, it's very easy to find yourself in a spiral of stress and emotions. It can feel as if everything is up in the air. A grounding ritual will help to bring you back to the present moment, and remind you that you are rooted and connected to the earth.

One of the simplest ways to feel grounded is to just take off your shoes and stand or walk on the earth – outside on grass is best, if that's possible. Close your eyes and think about your connection to the ground beneath your feet. Feel as if you have roots growing from the soles of your feet, all the way deep into the earth. Concentrate on your breath. It may feel a bit silly at first, but it is a surprisingly powerful practice for calming yourself down.

We spend so much of our lives disconnected from the earth by chairs or shoes or buildings, that some experts in grounding (sometimes it's called earthing) say that you should stand barefoot on the earth outside for an hour a day to balance yourself out. This is going to be way easier if you live by a beach somewhere tropical, but for the rest of us, a few minutes on the nearest patch of earth will do.

If you're feeling brave, go all out and lie flat on the grass. Spread yourself out like a starfish and feel your whole body release and connect with the ground.

A RITUAL FOR PROTECTION

When we're feeling threatened by change, we can feel bombarded from all sides. This ritual will allow you to feel protected and safe, no matter what is happening around you.

For this ritual you will need a large piece of plain paper and a marker pen.

You're going to draw a symbol on the paper, large enough to surround your feet if you were standing on the paper.

Here are some symbols that we like to use:

The evil eye This ancient symbol of a vivid blue eye, with winged eyeliner, often seen in Greece and Egypt, is believed to protect you from the bad intentions of others.

The hamsa You may have seen this symbol of an outstretched right hand, sometimes with an eye at the centre of the palm; it's commonly used in the Middle East. It is said to offer blessing and also protection from negative intent.

A peace sign The commonly used peace sign of a circle with a vertical line and two smaller diagonal lines was originally created for the British Campaign for Nuclear Disarmament. It was taken up by hippies in the Sixties as a symbol of the counterculture, and is now widely used around the world.

Earth medicine wheel This Native American symbol is simply a circle, divided into quarters by a cross. The quarters of the wheel are said to represent the four seasons and the four elements, and to promote harmony and peaceful interaction between all beings.

Once you've drawn your chosen symbol, place the paper on the ground and stand on the paper with your feet planted firmly on the ground.

Stand with your arms down by your sides, palms facing forward (rather than in towards the body).

Inhale and raise your arms overhead, so that your palms touch. As you exhale, keep the palms together and bring the hands down in prayer position, silently saying to yourself, '*I am safe and protected*'. Repeat for at least one minute, then stay standing in your protective symbol for as long as feels comfortable.

OBSERVING CHANGE

When we're in the middle of upheavals in our life, big or small, things can feel chaotic and overwhelming, and we have no sense of a bigger picture or a grand plan. In these times, the simplest thing you can do is just pay attention to where you are right now.

Keep a journal and write down not just what is happening day to day, but how you feel, too. You don't have to be Pollyanna-ish about this and only write down the good stuff, get it all down – the happy and the sad.

Do this every day, no excuses! The act of writing down your feelings allows you to stay present and still when it feels like everything else is moving too fast. You will begin to see patterns to your emotions, and how you can change the way you respond. Over time, and with attention, you'll recognise the hole in the street, instead of falling into it again.

With a consistent daily practice of observation you'll begin to see that the situation that felt so all-consuming has been changing all along, and so have you.

GANESH, REMOVER OF OBSTACLES

In the Hindu tradition, the deity Ganesh (or Ganesha) is revered as the remover of obstacles. He is easily recognised, as he has the head of an elephant and the body of a boy and rides around on a tiny mouse. When you get right into the philosophy of it, Ganesh is not just the remover of obstacles, but also the god who places the right obstacles in front of you, so that you can overcome them and achieve your highest potential.

Our dad experienced a lot of obstacles in his life, and maybe that's why he really loved Ganesh. He collected statues of him for years, and once even carried a huge stone and gold Ganesh all the way from India to Hong Kong (it now lives in Katia's garden).

We both have Ganesh statues in our homes – Nadia keeps hers by the front door for protection and good fortune. At times when we need a little extra help, we make an offering to Ganesh of a little dish of water, some flowers and a lit candle. We ask him to remove our obstacles, and to trust that the ones that are there will teach us the lessons we need to learn.

A Ganesh statue or figure is also a really great present to give to someone who's going through a hard time.

SPEAKING YOUR TRUTH

Sometimes change only comes because we ask for it. It's important that we are not silent about things that matter. Women in particular are often encouraged to be quiet and to not make others feel uncomfortable. Withholding our voices and our desire for change can lead us to feel blocked and angry.

Speaking your truth does not mean being harsh or aggressive, though a voice that has long been blocked may initially emerge that way. Most of us have had the experience of keeping quiet about an experience that has hurt us, and then exploding with anger about something small and unrelated!

Being more in touch with our thoughts and emotions helps us to recognise times when we might be bottling things up. Rather than giving vent to your anger, consider how you might articulate your truth in a manner that is honest and vulnerable. This invites connection and community, instead of argument.

Opening the throat, where the voice is said to come from, can help dissolve those blockages and leave us free to speak the truth, for ourselves and for others. If we want change, we have to speak up. Let this ritual help you find your voice.

* Put a drop of lavender essential oil on your palms (lavender is the oil of truth and communication) and rub them together. Inhale deeply over your cupped hands for three breaths.

* Bring your attention to your throat, open your mouth and take three deep breaths in and out of your mouth, focusing on the centre of your throat.

* Use a crystal that is associated with honesty – we like lapis lazuli and amazonite. Hold the crystal at your throat while counting your inhale for four, and your exhale for four.

* Inhale, scrunch up your face really tight, and on the exhale open your eyes and your mouth wide and stick your tongue out with a loud roar. In yoga this is called lion's breath. Repeat three times.

* Repeat an affirmation that resonates with you; we like to say, '*I am grateful for my voice, and the freedom to use it to speak my truth.*'

There are times when speaking our truth is not possible. If you think your boss is an idiot, it's not going to be a great idea to tell them so. If a person close to you is not ready to hear you, it may be the case that you should speak to someone else instead, such as a therapist. There is power in speaking your truth out loud, even if it's not to the person directly.

If therapy is not an option, perhaps because it's unaffordable, write your thoughts down in a letter, and then read it out loud. When you're done, rip the letter up, or burn it, and release the heavy feelings that you've been holding on to.

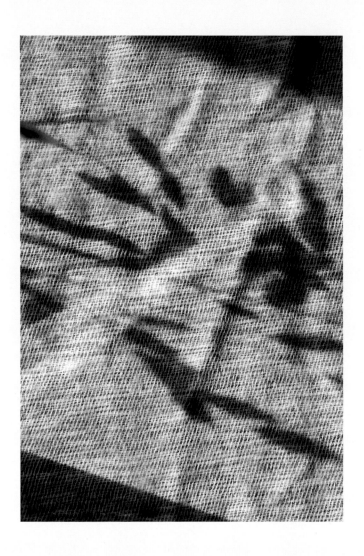

PAUSE and consider if the change you are experiencing is one you welcomed, or one that caught you by surprise. Can you find a way to welcome, with gratitude, both kinds of change?

PAY ATTENTION to how change makes you feel. Does it make you grip tightly to how things are? Can you loosen your hold and learn to let go?

SET YOUR INTENTION to flow with changes as they come, and to recognise them as part of the ever-changing cycle of life.

accepting

'God grant me the serenity to accept the things I cannot change, courage to change the things I can, and wisdom to know the difference.' *Reinhold Niebur*

One of our favourite teachings comes from our friend Vinny Ferraro, who likes to say, 'Right now, it's like this'. It's a line we remind ourselves of when we forget that life's plans for us might be different to our own.

When we find ourselves in difficult situations, we often have the urge to fix them – we want to find the answer or solution that will make things better. But sometimes the solution is just to sit with the way things are, instead of trying to change them.

Acceptance is not the same as denial, or avoidance, and it doesn't mean that we give up or lose hope. Instead, acceptance is about digging deep down to embrace life exactly as it is right now.

You can live your life waiting for that apology, or you can move on, accepting that it's never going to happen. Weirdly, once you accept things it can sometimes be easier to change them – sometimes we just get tired of our own bullshit.

BEING WITH THINGS AS THEY ARE

True, radical acceptance is a positive choice to focus on the good in our lives. It's a really hard choice sometimes, and we're not denying that. It takes work and effort, and it can be pretty uncomfortable.

But think about what you could do with all the time and energy you're currently spending on resisting the life you're in. Acceptance is a kind of beautiful honesty about where we are right now, and learning to lean into that can be incredibly liberating.

JUST SIT

This ritual sounds so simple you might want to skip over to one with candles and crystals that sounds more fun. Don't! Learning to be with things as they are, without any attachment or aversion, is a Buddhist practice that can have a profound effect.

Buddhists often call meditation 'sitting', because really that's all you need to do. It doesn't need to be complicated, so don't let the idea intimidate you.

* Find a quiet and comfortable place where you won't be disturbed, and set a timer for five minutes.

* Close your eyes and really focus on the noises around you. What can you hear? Maybe a plane flying overhead? A car passing in the street outside? Pay attention to every single sound, even the very subtle flow of your own breathing. Let the sounds you hear bring you right into the present moment.

* Feel the sensations in your body. Are you warm? Cold? Is there a breeze? Is one of your legs getting pins and needles from sitting cross-legged? The body will want to fidget to get away from how you're feeling but stay still. Just sit with these feelings exactly as they are.

* Now pay attention to your thoughts, which will probably be jumping all around, trying to distract you. This is sometimes called the 'monkey mind', as it's always grasping for something new. Don't judge your thoughts, or feel that you ought to be thinking about something pure and spiritual. Just be with your mind as it is right now, with all of its craziness.

Sounds simple, right? Trust us, this one is really bloody hard to do. When Katia first studied Vipassana meditation she found it so difficult she literally escaped from the retreat and hitch-hiked away!

Learning to sit with discomfort – whether that's distracting sensations or annoying noises – is the first step to being able to sit with bigger and more uncomfortable situations when they arise.

ACCEPTING YOURSELF

When things don't go right for us – the relationship doesn't work out, the dream job goes to someone else, we totally mess something up – we can find ourselves overcome with a sense of shame. Shame is one of the most uncomfortable emotions out there. Most of us will allow ourselves to feel negative emotions like sadness (who doesn't feel the benefit of a good cry?), but we'll do pretty much anything to avoid that burning sense of self-loathing.

When we battle with blame and recrimination we remind ourselves of the great Maya Angelou quote: 'You did then what you knew how to do, and when you knew better, you did better.'

Accepting the sense of shame, instead of running from it, is the first step to being more compassionate towards yourself.

We've adapted this ritual from a Jewish ceremony that is performed on the afternoon of Rosh Hashanah. In this tradition bread is cast into the water, to represent casting away your sins.

You can use bread for this ritual, if you like, but we prefer to use a twig or a small branch instead, as we like the feeling of returning our feelings to nature. Make sure your branch is something small and light – not a huge stick – as the idea is that it will float away instead of sinking.

You will need to find some running water outside, such as a stream, or river, or even the sea.

Take some time to arrive at your place by the water. Inhale a few deep breaths and think about your intentions. Hold the leaves or branch in your hand, and address all of your feelings of shame and fear towards them. It's so much better to acknowledge these feelings instead of trying to escape them.

Expressing your negative thoughts out loud is best, as often these things sound much less significant when you hear them rather than think them. But in your head is fine if you're worried about being overheard.

When you've really let it all out, throw the twig or branch into the water and let it float away.

As you watch it go, remind yourself that every difficult situation and emotion will also pass.

CIRCULAR BREATHING

At times when we feel totally under siege, our first reaction to the suggestion of a breathing exercise can be, 'Breathing? *Please.* Someone get me a Valium.'

Bestselling author Brené Brown tells a great story about how she resisted the idea of breathing exercises for years, thinking they were pointless and couldn't possibly work, until finally she asked a Navy SEAL how he kept calm in situations of extreme and life-threatening pressure. His answer? The breathing exercise below.

You can do this ritual anywhere – at work, on public transport, or in the car. No one will be able to tell you're doing it, so remember that pausing and paying attention are possible anywhere.

* Inhale to a count of four

* Hold the breath to a count of four

* Exhale to a count of four

* Hold the exhalation to a count of four

* Repeat for a full minute, or more

If it works for a Navy SEAL, it just might work for you too.

RADICAL ACCEPTANCE

This one can be a bit tricky, as we're asking you to be grateful for the situation that is causing you pain. You'll need a notebook, a pen and a willingness to look beyond the immediate moment.

Take a moment to think about the situation you're facing. Radical acceptance means welcoming it in – all of it, even the bits that are the most sticky and painful and difficult. *Especially* those bits.

Here's an example:

'Thank you for helping me accept that my relationship ended for the right reasons, even if I can't see them yet. Thank you for the gift of this pain, which is allowing me to be vulnerable and open. Thank you for revealing the people who show up for me and care for me in these moments. Thank you for reminding me that I am loved when I feel unlovable.'

Our worst times can be our greatest teachers, if we'll allow it.

DIFFICULT PEOPLE

We all have to deal with difficult people, and sometimes, let's face it, *we're* the difficult person. When we're really finding someone hard to deal with, we try to remind ourselves that we never know what someone else is going through.

Remember that the voice a person uses with others is a just a pale reflection of the voice they're using with themselves. If that voice is harsh to you, it's probably way harsher to themselves, and that deserves our compassion.

If we react to the harsh voice, instead of the hurt person behind it, they are likely to become defensive, which just makes the situation worse. We can't change a person's behaviour – only they can do that – but we can try to accept where their feelings might be coming from.

This is not an easy ritual to practice. It needs constant repetition and reinforcement to overcome our natural tendency to retaliate against those who are aggressive to us. And we have to admit, we don't always succeed in overcoming the urge to shout back! But when we do succeed in responding with kindness, we're reminded of how approaching others with love and compassion can defuse a charged situation. A considered response can bring us, and the other person, a little closer towards finding common ground.

As the late British politician Jo Cox reminded us, no matter how far apart our beliefs and behaviours may be, as humans we have more in common than that which divides us. In these polarised times, reminding ourselves of our shared humanity can only be a good thing.

* Instead of snapping back, pause for a moment. Take a breath.

* Think of that person as a tiny baby, in the arms of their mother. Really focus on them as small, vulnerable and innocent.

* Think of the baby crying because of some feeling it can't express – hunger, thirst or tiredness. When a baby cries we understand that it is expressing its emotions the only way it can. When an adult loses their cool, can we try to have compassion for the unexpressed feelings behind their behaviour?

* Notice how wrong it would feel to send anger and negativity towards such a tiny, helpless baby.

* Send the difficult person compassion and understanding. We recommend you do this in your head, as they may not be ready to hear this yet.

We'd also gently suggest there is nothing more annoying than being told to calm down if you're the person who's lost their temper! So bear that in mind and keep your behaviour compassionate instead of smug or self-congratulatory. This ritual is not about proving your superiority, it's about finding connection and understanding.

DIFFICULT SITUATIONS

When you can't change a situation, sometimes the very best you can do is just treat your anxiety around it. These rituals offer two really simple techniques to bring you back into your body. Try them in times when you're awake in the night because of worries, or if you're waking up full of fear at what the day ahead might hold.

* Pinch the index finger and the thumb of your right hand in the space between the index finger and thumb of your left hand (see picture). This is an acupressure technique that is great for calming the nervous system. If you want to amp this up, add a little essential oil and massage the space by squeezing your finger and thumb together. Lavender and bergamot are good for anxiety. Repeat on the other hand.

* In Chinese medicine, the space in the centre of the chest, just under the breastbone, is known as the 'sea of tranquillity'. This is the location of the thymus gland, which is part of the lymphatic system. Tapping the centre of the chest (sometimes called thymus thumping) is said to reduce stress and anxiety. Join all of your fingers and thumb together, as if you were holding a sock puppet, and use the fingertips to tap on the chest for about thirty seconds. Repeat two or three times a day.

REMEMBERING THE
THINGS THAT WERE

It can be bittersweet to recall the people or the happy times that we have lost. That mixture of joy and pain is something we often find uncomfortable, and try to push away.

When we repress our feelings of grief and sadness, we may be afraid to release them even a little bit, in case we're unable to put the cork back in the bottle. But if we allow ourselves to explore these emotions in a safe space, we may find them less frightening. And we may discover that we can remember the people and the times that have passed with happiness instead of sadness.

Rituals can help us find a space for these conflicting feelings, especially in situations where we may be afraid our emotions will get the better of us.

ANNIVERSARY RITUAL

Even after the immediate grief of losing a person or when a situation has passed, you're left with the tricky terrain of anniversaries. While time does make things easier, we both noticed in the years that followed our dad's death that we'd get a bit crazy as the anniversary approached.

These are a few rituals that we still practise to be kind to ourselves around this time. You can use these to commemorate a person or an event.

It's important to grant ourselves the space to accept the grief that will be coming our way, whether we make time for it or not.

* Look ahead in your diary – make a plan to be gentle to yourself that day, and in the surrounding days. If it's possible to take the day off work, give yourself some space to feel what comes up for you on the anniversary.

* When our dad was dying, Nadia wrote a journal that she re-reads every year around the anniversary. It reconnects her to that time and reminds her how her grief has changed over the years since.

* Light a candle for the person you've lost, or the situation you're mourning.

* Spend time with your family, remembering stories about your person or situation. Have a dinner together and leave an empty chair to represent the person who is no longer there.

* Plant a tree on the first anniversary. Every year afterwards you can visit the tree and tie a ribbon around the trunk, lay flowers, or attach photographs or letters to the branches.

COMMEMORATION AT CELEBRATIONS

If you have lost someone close to you, it can be hard to think about celebrating big events without them. This can be really difficult if you are getting married without the parent you had hoped would be there, or facing a christening without a beloved grandparent or dear friend.

At these times it can feel strange or inappropriate to have a sense of mourning in the middle of what is supposed to be a happy day. We can feel conflicted about how to both celebrate the joyful occasion and acknowledge the sense of loss we may be feeling.

These are two small rituals that we've experienced at the celebrations of our friends, and which we've felt were subtle and sensitive.

* At an appropriate moment in a wedding celebration, the couple can pause and announce that they are lighting a candle for those who can't be with them today. To guests who know about the family's loss, this has meaning, and to everyone else it's just a nice moment that doesn't necessarily hold any sad connotations.

* Make a commemoration tree. Place a large branch in a vase and leave it somewhere at the event together with ribbons, scissors and gift tags. Invite guests to write their memories and their wishes on to the cards and to tie them to the branch. This is a space for celebration, and also for commemoration, if liked.

TRUST WHAT IS

There is a great saying that when one door closes another door opens, but the corridor is a bitch. Although we want to believe everything will turn out okay, it's much harder to feel that way when it seems as if we're stuck in the corridor with all the doors around us slammed shut.

When a door closes in our faces, it's common to stare at that door for a long time, wondering what happened. We pick over the bones of the situation, replaying conversations, and questioning how we missed signs that now seem obvious. We dredge up ancient arguments and start to create new, often mistaken, stories around old relationships.

Trust and acceptance of what is asks us to look away from the closed door, so we can open our eyes to what else is out there. Accepting what is happening, instead of fighting it, gives us an inner resilience that helps us navigate the peaks and troughs of everyday life.

We like to think of these rituals as a kind of cushion that will soften your landing and help you get back up again.

ACCEPTING THE GOOD STUFF

So often we focus on our failings rather than our successes. It seems to come much easier to beat ourselves up than to congratulate ourselves. It can even feel wrong to acknowledge when things are going well – like we're setting ourselves up for a fall.

But showing off is not the same as being proud of yourself. Showing off is about getting the approval of others, being proud is about pausing to recognise for ourselves the times when we've achieved something great.

Sometimes when things are going well for us, we feel we're too busy to stop and appreciate the moment. We panic that if we stop, our luck will disappear. While we agree you've got to keep working hard, it's so important to make time to be proud and grateful.

Have you ever noticed how we spend so much of our lives wishing for things, and once we get them, our minds leap on to the next want or need?

* Pause right now and remind yourself of something you've done really well.

* Write down all the things you did that made it happen. Remember the moments in the process when you doubted yourself, and remind yourself that you achieved it anyway.

* If you're feeling especially fortunate, pass on some of that good fortune. We like donating to microfinance charities, which help entrepreneurs around the world to achieve their goals. Passing on a bit of your luck is a way of giving thanks for it.

THE TRUST WALK

We learned this ritual from our teacher, Gurmukh, when we studied with her in California. It can be a difficult one for some of us, especially if we have trust issues. The harder it is, the more you need to do it.

You will need a trusted friend for this ritual, as well as a blindfold and a safe space in which to walk.

Have your friend blindfold you, then take a short walk, letting your friend guide you. Notice how hard it is for you to trust another person, and how often you want to open your eyes and sneak a peek. Instead really try to lean into those feelings of wanting to be in control, and see if you can fully trust the person who is leading you.

Make sure that your friend gives you enough guidance to allow you to relax into the trust walk. They should let you know if you're navigating around a tree, for example, or if you're about to take a step up on to the pavement. Working out how much guidance you need is a good exercise in trust for both you and your friend.

FINDING PEACE

There is an old Zen story about a young monk who was struggling to learn to meditate. He went to his master and complained, 'Every time I try to meditate, a dog starts barking outside. It barks the whole time, and I can't concentrate. If I could just get rid of the dog, everything would be fine.' The master thought for a moment and asked, 'Does the dog come into the room to bark at you? Or do you leave the room to be barked at by it?'

Peace is a bit like this. We tell ourselves that it's not our fault we don't feel peaceful – it's the fault of our job, our relationship or the place where we live. Or we can make the mistake of thinking that peace is something we'll find by going on holiday, or getting out into nature. In other words, that it's something outside of ourselves, to be found somewhere other than where we already are. We think we'd feel peaceful if only everything was a little less difficult and frustrating.

But is life frustrating us, or are we going outside of ourselves to be frustrated by it? If we learn to accept things as they are, then we remove those layers of annoyance and resistance – we get rid of the barking dog – and we find that peace was there underneath all along.

Real peace means finding space in the everyday, instead of waiting for the picture-postcard version of our lives where everything is perfect.

SILENT RITUAL

On Nadia's yoga retreats everyone observes a silence in the mornings. At first people find it a bit strange not to chat to each other over breakfast, especially as they feel they should be polite and friendly, but in time it becomes many people's favourite part of the week. That restful start is carried with them through the rest of the day.

Try making a pact with the people you live with that you won't talk for the first half hour of the day. If they're not up for it, just get up a bit earlier yourself for that silent time. And if you live alone, keep the radio or television switched off and allow your home to be quiet.

Don't think only about speech when it comes to silence. In the Vipassana tradition, practising silence is extended to everything that you're doing. So think about how you're navigating in space – put your cup down quietly, close cupboard doors softly, move slowly.

Being quiet and still in your movements invites that stillness into your mind.

BATH SALTS FOR PEACE

Taking a bath is a great way to bring a moment of peace and calm to your life. Try to resist the temptation to turn every bath into a 'doing' space, where you're reading or putting on a face mask or shaving your legs. Every now and again, let your bath be a 'being' space, where you just lie quietly. A candlelit bath is great for this, as it's hard to read in the dark.

These bath salts will last for ages in a glass jar and they make a lovely present – who wouldn't want to bathe in a little peace?

BASE RECIPE

- 2 cups Epsom salts
- I cup salt (we use pink Himalayan)
- 10–15 drops of essential oils (see below)

Calming and uplifting
5 drops of lavender, 5 drops of geranium

Relaxing
5 drops of cedarwood, 5 drops of ylang ylang (both of these oils are natural sedatives)

Anxiety-relieving
5 drops of lavender, 3 drops of neroli, 3 drops of rose

These are some of our favourite essential oil blends to add for peaceful baths – just stir them in until well mixed. Start with ten drops, in case your skin is sensitive, and go up to fifteen drops if you'd like a stronger scent.

A CRYSTAL GRID FOR PEACE

When it comes to peace, these are the crystals that we like to have in our homes as a reminder to tap into that feeling whenever we can.

Amethyst for peace and tranquillity.

Clear quartz the master healer.

Petrified wood for patience and trusting in the flow of life.

If you want to step it up a notch, you can try making a crystal grid; having a number of crystals leading to your central crystal is said to create a stronger and quicker result.

* Choose the central crystal that you would like to use (see page 184 for ideas). Write your intention for peace (or anything else – this ritual is super adaptable) on some paper and place it under the central crystal.

* Surround your central crystal with a circle of smaller stones, perhaps five or six of them. These are called your way stones; they create the path to your desire. Choose small pebble crystals, whichever ones resonate with you.

* The third element of the grid is an outer circle of stones, called the desire stones. These represent the desired outcome. Again, use small crystals here.

* Finally, take a clear quartz crystal to activate your grid. This means getting quiet and concentrating on your intention. Then link all the stones together by simply using the clear quartz to draw an invisible line connecting each stone to every other stone, and to the central crystal.

PAUSE and consider the situations that you struggle to accept. Ask yourself what it is that you are resisting.

PAY ATTENTION to how resistance makes you feel. Can you sense it in your body? Perhaps your chest is tight, or your breathing shallow? How does it feel to sit with that uncomfortable feeling and just let it be? Does the sensation change if you breathe more deeply?

SET YOUR INTENTION to accept, today, one thing that you can't change. Thank the uncomfortable situation for everything it is bringing to you, the things that you can't yet see.

ending

'In the end, only three things matter: how much you loved, how gently you lived, and how gracefully you let go of things not meant for you.' *Jack Kornfield*

We often struggle to let go of the past, but to truly move forwards means accepting, and even embracing, the end. Some endings are big, some are small, some we resist and some we allow.

It feels so easy to welcome the end when it's something we're glad to see the back of – like terrible jobs or bad relationships. Yet it's so much harder to get to grips with the endings of things we'd hoped would last.

Part of embracing the end is understanding that nothing is forever; not the good stuff, and not the bad. It is only our attachment that makes endings feel so hard. We have to learn to let go of our grip on the outcome, and release the situation with grace.

Times of loss often leave us feeling that everything is out of control. Rituals, especially those with deliberate steps and stages to follow, can help to counter that sense of helplessness by giving us a place and a time for our grief.

We want to warn you that some of these rituals might make you feel sad – and that's okay. Letting your sadness happen is the start of letting it go.

BEREAVEMENT

We're starting with the big one, the real, final ending that no one gets to escape.

Rituals give us permission to process our grief, and a safe space in which to allow ourselves to fully feel the emotions. There are big traditional rituals around grief, such as funerals or sitting shiva for seven days, and these can act as milestones for public grieving.

But when those public occasions are over, life goes on for everyone else, while it might feel as if it has stopped for you. This can be a lonely time in the grieving process, when you are afraid to burden others with the depth of your emotions. We'd encourage you to find a good friend you can speak to if you're in this situation; the people who love you will want to be there for you. Let them.

In quieter times, small, personal rituals can help you through those moments of grief when you may feel lost and alone.

WEARING MOURNING

In Victorian times, a person who had lost a loved one would dress in black to show they were in mourning. In later years this became a black armband instead of entirely black clothing, and occasionally you still see people wearing these. In Asian cultures, the colour of mourning is white – our Indian grandmother always wore a white sari after our grandfather died.

In modern life we tend to mourn privately. The people around us, unless we know them well, don't know that we are grieving. And it's a strange feeling, because you are walking around in the world with this huge hole of loss and grief and yet no one can tell from the outside.

We often think it would be so much easier if everyone could wear something to let those around them know they're suffering. It would make us all so much kinder to each other. But unless you want to make a badge to tell everyone you're grieving, we think you probably have to make a smaller gesture that's meaningful to you.

*   Carry an object, or a few objects, relating to the person who has died. Some people keep their husband's wallet in their bag, or a loved one's favourite pen.

*   Wear a piece of their jewellery, or their clothing. In the year after our father's death, whenever we really missed him, we'd wear his old pyjamas to bed and it made us feel connected to him.

Wearing or carrying something to remind yourself of your lost person is also a reminder to be kind and gentle with yourself at this time.

You may find over time that you no longer feel the need to have the clothing or the jewellery or the object with you all the time, and you will know from this that you have moved through the first and hardest part of the grieving process.

AN ALTAR TO YOUR LOST PERSON

Although it might sound a little morbid, creating an altar or a shrine to the person you have lost is a way of keeping them close when it feels like they've gone forever.

An altar for grief will be personal to you and the person you are grieving, but these are some ideas for things you might add.

* Photographs of your person, plus objects that had meaning to you and them. Perhaps their watch or a piece of their jewellery.

* Rosemary has been the traditional herb for remembrance since Roman times, when it was used in burial rites. Add sprigs to your altar, or just tuck them into a framed picture of the person who has died.

* A rose quartz crystal is good for a broken heart, while amethyst is said to help you to absorb pain and grief.

* You can diffuse essential oils on your altar – we love melissa, which is good for depression. Orange oil is uplifting and helps bring joy to your heart when you may feel there's not much joy to be had.

* A candle. Light the candle each day and sit at your altar for as long as feels comfortable to you. Let yourself feel whatever comes up.

In the Buddhist tradition, ceremonies are performed for forty-nine days after a death. We like to follow this tradition by sitting at our altar each day for this period, as it's a long enough time frame to really get into your feelings, but please do what feels right to you – don't feel bad if you need to perform your ritual for a longer or shorter time.

HERBAL TEA FOR GRIEF

Hawthorn has been used in many cultures as a traditional remedy for grief and heartbreak. It is said to offer protection, especially for the heart. Our friend, herbalist Michael Istead, uses the berries as the basis of a special herbal tea for times of grief. This makes a beautiful gift for a friend who is mourning a loved one.

You can find dried hawthorn berries online or in herbal shops (please consult a doctor before using if you are on any heart medications).

We find that the ceremony of creating the tea with intention, and sipping it, is as comforting as the tea itself.

TO MAKE ONE JAR

- 1 cup dried hawthorn berries
- 1 cup dried rose petals (rose is believed to have properties that help to keep the heart open, instead of closing in on itself)
- 1 cup tulsi leaves (also known as holy basil, tulsi is known in India as the 'Queen of Herbs' for its stress-relieving properties)

Use one teaspoonful of tea per cup, pour over boiling water and leave to steep for a few minutes before drinking.

TENSION RELEASE

On the African savannah, when a zebra has escaped from a lion, you will see that afterwards its entire body twitches and vibrates. This is the release of the tension from its body, as the zebra calms down from the intense fight or flight response.

Humans, too, hold tension in the body from traumatic events, but unlike the zebra, we don't usually physically process it. When we hold on to tension in the body, we are left feeling stressed and anxious.

You don't need to be faced with a lion to experience trauma. The daily grind of noise, stress, pressure and deadlines over a long period of time can build up to have as much impact as one significant, stressful event.

Here is a ritual that will help release some of that stuck tension and grief from your body. It seems really simple, but releasing tension doesn't have to be complicated – if a zebra can do it, so can you.

* Start by standing with your feet hip width apart.

* Bend your knees and just start bouncing gently up and down. Make sure the body is relaxed and not stiff.

* Taking deep breaths, let the bounce reverberate through your body. Feel the bounce travel up from your feet into your pelvis and up your spine.

* Lift your arms above your head for a few breaths and shake out the wrists and hands. Feel the bounce release your shoulders, then relax your arms down by your sides.

* Inhale deeply then release a deep loud sigh. Do this at least three times.

* Then inhale again, and exhale with a loud *aaaahh* or *huaaaahhh* sound a few times.

Keep bouncing for at least five minutes and let your body guide you to where the tension most needs releasing. When the time is up, slow it down, take some deep breaths and pause to feel the effect of the vibration in your body.

If you're somewhere where no one can hear you (and where no one's going to call the police thinking something terrible's happened) it can also be really freeing to let yourself scream and shout.

SAYING GOODBYE

It's strange how hard it can be to accept that something is over when it hasn't truly gone away. The abrupt shock of bereavement can feel almost preferable to the confusing swirl of emotions around rejection – whether you're the one being rejected or doing the rejection.

Perhaps you're struggling with the end of a relationship, romantic or otherwise, that has simply run its course. It might be a job you had to get away from, or a bad living situation. Heartbreak comes in many forms.

Despite what we might have heard, not all relationships need that moment of closure with the other person. You won't always get the response you want from someone else. Sometimes it is wiser for you to acknowledge and define the end for yourself, by yourself, so that you can let it go.

END OF RELATIONSHIP RITUAL

When you break up with someone, whether that's a friend or a partner, it can feel that the conversation just seems to stop. If you are the person who's been rejected you may feel that there is still so much more to say, but the other person has stopped listening.

In this situation we like to write that person a letter – DO NOT post it! This letter is for you, not them. Take a few days to write this. Keep going back and adding to the letter. Make sure you've said it all and left nothing out.

Sit with the letter for a while, and maybe even put it on your altar. Give yourself a deadline for sitting at your altar and mourning your relationship. We suggest sitting for a few minutes every day for between twenty-one and forty days. It may take much less time if you are lucky.

In this time, keep adding to your letter, get the photographs out, play the songs that resonate with the relationship and really get to the heart of all the pain you're feeling.

Once the deadline is over, burn the letter and put away all of your photographs. If you've really taken time to sit with the pain, you'll be ready to move on.

NOSTALGIA

Having been born and raised in Hong Kong, we sometimes really miss the things that we were brought up with. Homesickness and nostalgia are so tightly linked – of course we can go back to Hong Kong, and we do, but no one can go back to the past.

At times when we feel that longing to reconnect with home we head straight for Chinatown to eat! Or we go to the Chinese supermarket and load up on the sweets and drinks that we were raised on. Katia likes to share these with her kids, along with the stories of our childhoods.

Weirdly, the foods that everyone seems to crave from childhood are the super-processed junk ones, like sweets and crisps, so in times of painful nostalgia, just give yourself a break and surrender into that without judgement.

You don't have to have lived abroad to feel like you have lost a time or a place that you will never get back. When the feeling of nostalgia hits, try this ritual to bring sweetness back into your memories.

Get a small cardboard box and take the time to cover it in images that remind you of the time you're missing – perhaps some newspapers, or photographs. Add to the box everything you have kept from that period: photos, notes and little things you have collected, and the (non-perishable) foods you loved. When you feel that need to connect to where you came from, open your box and enjoy your memories. It can also be very healing to share your memories with someone else.

CLOSURE

Taking time to acknowledge endings can help us to let things go. Sometimes well-meaning friends advise us to put things behind us, and move on before we're ready. We might even hear that it's not good to wallow in sad feelings.

We respectfully disagree that dealing with your feelings is wallowing. Moving on without achieving closure just means that your emotions will return later, and any therapist will tell you that it is harder and more confusing to deal with sadness or anger when it is no longer attached to the situation that caused it.

Rituals aren't magic spells that get rid of our feelings, but they do allow us to stop to acknowledge the passing of time, and of emotion, and that can help us to achieve a sense of closure.

CANDLE RITUAL

In Mexico you can buy lucky candles in tall glass jars, and it's said that if you write your wishes on the wax surface as you burn the candle away, your wish will come true. We like to use the same principle to say goodbye to the things we need to let go of.

Take a small candle (the bigger it is, the longer it will take to burn away, so keep it small), and use a pen or a skewer to write on the side of it the thing you want to let go of. It can just be a word, or a short sentence.

I release my anger.

I'm willing to let you go.

Once you've written your intention, set the candle in its holder and light it. You can either leave the candle to burn down all at once, or relight it over a series of days until it's disappeared.

Try not to just light the candle and then get busy doing other things. Instead, stay and watch it burn. Really focus on the sensation of releasing and letting go.

A CLOSING CIRCLE

When we've spent time with a group of people – perhaps on retreat or even on a holiday – we may want to find a way to mark the end of that experience. We're thinking of something a bit more meaningful than just being on a group text afterwards.

At the end of Nadia's retreats the group sits in a circle and takes it in turn to share their experiences of the week. In some Native American traditions a feather is passed around the circle to indicate who should speak, and we often use this.

You can adapt this ritual to any situation, from the end of a school year to a project you've been working on with other people. Just take an object – it doesn't have to be a feather – and pass it around the group, allowing people to speak in turn.

It can be very moving and it's a nice way to share the experience in the moment that it ends.

RITUAL FOR RELEASE

In situations where strong emotions arise, such as an argument with a family member or a particularly hard time at work, you may feel like you have taken on a heaviness and a stress that is not yours.

This can be particularly true if you work as a carer or a nurse, or in any job where you are deeply involved with people who are suffering. It is almost impossible not to be affected by the pain of others when you work closely with them.

At these times you may feel the need to release yourself from these heavy feelings.

Salt is considered the great neutraliser It helps to cleanse, balance and release negative energies. Simply take a handful of salt, dampen it with water, then scrub your hands clean over the sink. Rinse your hands under running water and say out loud, 'I release anything that doesn't belong to me.'

Light a sage stick or a piece of palo santo wood Both are known for their cleansing properties. Blow out the flame, then move the smoking stick around your body, especially around your head if you're overcome with thoughts and feelings.

Get outside The earth is strong and can absorb strong energies and emotions. Place your hands on the earth and ask it to absorb anything negative or heavy from you.

Salt water Danish author Isak Dinesen is quoted as saying that the cure for everything is salt water; whether tears, sweat or the sea. We can't all get into the ocean (though if you can, do it!), but we can pour a cupful of Epsom salts or sea salt into a bath. Add five drops of bergamot essential oil – said to relieve anxiety, fear and insecurity. Feel the heaviness release from your body as you float in the bath.

Black tourmaline This is the crystal associated with release and letting go. You can add this to your altar if you have made one, or just hold the stone in your palm and say, out loud, 'I release all that doesn't serve me.'

Throw a stone If you have to be in close proximity to someone who regularly brings you down, and it simply can't be avoided, you're going to need a stone. Not to throw at them, but to keep in your pocket or bag. Imagine sending all of your strong and heavy emotions into the stone. Let it hold all the feelings you would like to release. At the end of the day, or week, with this person, throw your stone far away, and say, out loud, 'This stone takes away my burden.' If you're feeling generous, you could add that the stone takes away the other person's burden, too.

GOOD NIGHT

The benefits of sleep go way beyond simply getting rid of the black rings under your eyes. Sleep is the most powerful healer for your body and mind; it is the time when your body repairs itself.

Sleep can lower your blood pressure, improve your mood, and even improve your body's immune response.

Being deprived of sleep is actually a torture technique. Try not to do this to yourself; sleep is one of the key pillars of good health, and you owe it to yourself to get a good night's rest.

SLEEP DRINKS

Oats contain melatonin, which relaxes you and makes you sleepy, so a cup of warm oat milk can be a good thing to drink before bed. Have it about an hour before you're ready, just as you're beginning to wind down for the night. After a while the ritual of making your bedtime drink will act as a signal to your body that it's time to relax.

Just heat up your oat milk and add one of the following.

* Chamomile is a natural herbal remedy for sleep. Steep a chamomile tea bag in the hot oat milk.

* Add a pinch of saffron strands to your hot oat milk; saffron is known to reduce anxiety and promote sleepiness.

* Ashwagandha is an adaptogenic herb famed for its ability to reduce stress and anxiety. Its Latin name, somnifera, means sleep-inducing. The powder tastes quite bitter, so we like to mix half a teaspoon of the powder with oat milk, half a teaspoon of rosewater and a teaspoon of honey to sweeten. If you're on any other medication, please check with your doctor before taking ashwagandha or any other adaptogen.

* Add a teaspoon of dried lavender flowers and leave to steep for five minutes.

PILLOW SPRAY

An essential oil pillow spray not only smells beautiful, a nightly ritual of spritzing it before bed can be calming. Turning down the sheets and misting a relaxing fragrance on to your pillows feels indulgent, and really helps you to wind down at the end of the day.

We also love to take a pillow spray when we travel – it helps a hotel room feel more like home.

All the essential oils we use in our spray are super-calming; vetiver is especially good for insomnia.

PILLOW SPRAY

- 80ml distilled water
- 10 drops of lavender essential oil
- 5 drops of chamomile essential oil
- 5 drops of vetiver essential oil

Combine and store in a glass spray bottle. Shake well before you spray over your pillow.

BEDTIME RITUAL

Every nerve in your body ends in your feet, so a reflexology massage before bed can help calm the nervous system and get you ready for sleep. We like to use lavender oil or Roman chamomile essential oils for this massage – you can use them neat or mix them with a little coconut oil, if you prefer. Both are renowned as sleep aids.

Putting essential oil on the soles of your feet is meant to be the quickest way to get the benefits into your bloodstream, as there are no sebaceous glands here and the pores are large, so the oil is absorbed faster.

Reflexologists use the feet as a map of the entire body. These maps can be very detailed, but broadly the toes relate to the head and brain, and the groove under each big toe represents the neck and shoulders. The ball of the foot is said to correspond with the chest, while the arch relates to the abdomen and digestive system. The heel and the ankle represent the reproductive organs, and the inside curve of each foot (above the arch) is said to mirror the spinal curve.

If you'd like more detail on reflexology maps, you can find plenty of them online.

* Begin by relaxing your feet, one at a time, by gently massaging and kneading them all over. Pay attention to any areas of pain or tension. Wiggle the feet and circle the ankle joints.

* Massage the outside edges of your big toes. This is said to help with the release of melatonin, the sleep hormone. Start at the base of the big toe, and rub up and down the edge of each toe.

* Then massage the inside crease of the big toe (where the toe meets the ball of the foot), a spot that is good for the release of tension, especially in the neck and shoulders.

* Move your thumb to the centre of the ball of your foot, just above the arch. This is the solar plexus centre; massage here for a sense of peace and relaxation.

* End your reflexology massage with a minute of 'breeze strokes' – running your fingers lightly up and down the tops, sides and bottoms of the feet. It should feel as if you were stroking your feet gently with a feather. This is said to be very calming for the nervous system.

It is often claimed that the deeply relaxed state people experience after a reflexology massage makes them especially open and receptive to positive suggestions. If you believe in affirmations, then this is a great time to say them to yourself, and really let them sink in. If you've done this massage on someone else, use your power of suggestion wisely!

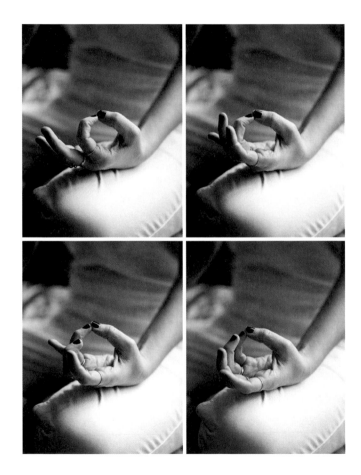

SA TA NA MA MEDITATION

We love this calming and stress-relieving Kundalini meditation before bed. Even Katia's eight-year-old has taken to doing this each night.

In the Kundalini tradition, the words Sa Ta Na Ma are the five primal sounds that represent the cycle of life, from beginning to end. Sa represents birth, Ta life, Na death or transformation and Ma rebirth.

* Tap the index figure with your thumb as you say the word SA

* Tap the middle finger with your thumb as you say the word TA

* Tap the ring finger with your thumb as you say the word NA

* Tap the baby finger to your thumb as you say the word MA

* Repeat for six minutes

* For the first minute, say the words out loud

* The second minute, whisper

* The third and fourth minute say the words silently to yourself

* The fifth minute, whisper

* For the final minute, say the words out loud again

If you're sharing the bed with someone else, you can always do the entire meditation silently.

PAUSE and consider the ending that you are facing.

PAY ATTENTION to how this ending is making you feel. Can you let go of the idea of a good ending and a bad ending? Can you release thoughts of blame – of others, and of yourself?

SET YOUR INTENTION to embrace the ending exactly as it is, and yourself exactly as you are.

We hope these simple rituals have given you some inspiration for ways to slow down the pace of your life, and to connect more deeply with the world around you.

Once you get comfortable with the idea of rituals, try creating some of your own. You don't have to be spiritual or woo woo to do this, you just have to be open and curious. Have fun creating the rituals that work for your own life.

Remember that rituals are simply a tool, they aren't an answer in themselves. Pausing, paying attention and setting clear intentions will bring you closer to your inner wisdom. You already have the answers you need, if you can just get quiet enough to hear them.

Lastly, we don't claim to be the experts on rituals, we're just two people who have found these techniques bring us moments of peace in a world that is often far from peaceful. We hope they might do the same for you.

10 ESSENTIAL OILS FOR BEGINNERS

Nadia has a huge shelf of essential oils at home, and she's got one for pretty much everything you could imagine. But she's been using these for years, and we know that starting out with essential oils can feel quite intimidating, so we've chosen the ten oils we'd recommend as a starter kit.

There are a couple of rules that apply to use of all essential oils. Please don't use them in food or drink unless they're certified food-grade oils. Don't use citrus oils on your face or in the sun, as they can cause skin reactions. Keep all neat essential oils away from your eyes. And if you're pregnant, or on medication, please consult your doctor before using any essential oils.

It's best to dilute essential oils with a carrier oil before use; we recommend either coconut or sweet almond oils.

LAVENDER

* If you only buy one essential oil, this is the one
* Reduces stress
* Calming
* Excellent for anxiety
* Encourages honesty and good communication
* Helps with sleep
* Good for burns on the skin and treatment of itchy insect bites

LEMON

* Keeps your mind focused, so it's a great one for aiding studying or concentration
* Clears the mind of negative thoughts and brings positive ones to the forefront
* Brings joy and happiness

FRANKINCENSE

* This oil is expensive, but worth it
* Grounding
* An anti-anxiety and antidepressant oil
* Helps reduce inflammation and is amazing for the skin
* Makes you feel loved and protected

TEA TREE/MELALEUCA

* The best disinfectant/hand sanitiser
* Antiseptic for minor cuts and wound.
* A good one to add to cleaning products in the home
* Clears negative energy and baggage and keeps energetic boundaries

PEPPERMINT

* Uplifting (it is often called the oil of the buoyant heart)
* Gives you a reprieve from emotional trials
* Helps you feel optimistic
* Freshens breath (food-grade only, please)
* Rub a drop on your temples to clear headaches and migraines (but don't use near your eyes)

BERGAMOT

* Uplifting
* Good for anxiety and depression
* Encourages confidence and hope

OREGANO

* Along with tea tree, this should be part of your medicine cabinet
* Considered a natural antibiotic

* Good for any kind of athlete's foot or toe fungus
* Also a good oil for remaining teachable and flexible with a willingness to be wrong

SANDALWOOD

* A good oil for relaxation
* A grounding oil, excellent for meditation and prayer
* Good for the skin – you can add a few drops to a carrier oil or face cream
* An aphrodisiac

GRAPEFRUIT

* Mood lifter
* Stimulates the immune system
* Helps with sugar cravings, and it's a good hangover cure!

ROMAN CHAMOMILE

* Excellent for anxiety and depression
* One of the best oils for insomnia
* Helps soothe cramps and muscle ache related to PMS

10 CRYSTALS
FOR BEGINNERS

We totally get that crystals are considered to be quite out there, and we'd never try to push them on anyone, but personally we love them. Even sceptics can agree that they're not going to do you any harm.

You can take the information below with a pinch of salt or, if you're interested to know more, there are plenty of detailed guides out there.

These are the ten crystals that we use most often and that we recommend to our friends and the people we work with.

AMETHYST

* Said to bring peace and tranquillity to the home, and is calming for the mind
* Creates a protective shield that wards off negative energy. Katia's son Huxley sleeps with a small amethyst under his pillow

BLACK OBSIDIAN

* Shields you against negativity, and absorbs negativity in the environment
* Always in Nadia's pocket

ROSE QUARTZ

* The ultimate heart healer
* The stone of love towards yourself and others
* A great wedding or new baby gift

CLEAR QUARTZ

* Brings clarity of mind and clears confusion
* Assists in clear communication
* Excellent for meditation

SUN PYRITE

* The stone of manifestation and taking action to create abundance in your life
* Brings mental clarity

SMOKY QUARTZ

* Grounding
* Offers protection from electromagnetic fields and computers.
* Keep one on your desk near the router

TITANIUM AURA QUARTZ

* The most powerful and highest vibration of all quartz
* Helps you to be grounded, centred and energised all at once

TIGER'S EYE

* Keeps you grounded and calm, regardless of the situation
* Gives the carrier strength in difficult situations
* Katia's kids carry these in their pockets

CARNELIAN

* Helps with taking big leaps of faith and action to manifest your dreams
* Promotes positive life choices and success
* A good one to add to a manifesting altar

CITRINE

* Said to boost the energy of the other crystals around it
* Great for manifestation, prosperity and abundance

ACKNOWLEDGEMENTS

First and foremost we would like to thank Pippa Wright, without whom there would be no second (or first!) book. Pippa, you have been the best editor two girls could dream of having. You push us and believe in us in ways we have never experienced from anyone. Thank you is not big enough. You have made our dreams come true (again). Please don't ever stop!

Thank you to Jocasta Hamilton, Celeste Ward-Best, Elle Gibbons, Rachel Kennedy, Najma Finlay and Becky McCarthy at Hutchinson for being the best publishing team we could have – both times around. You make writing books fun!

Thank you Viki Ottewill for the gorgeous cover, and to Abi Hartshorne for another perfect book design.

We were so glad to work with Issy Croker and her assistant Steph McLeod on the photographs. Thank you for taking a chance and trying something different with us, and for all the energy and ideas you both brought to the shoot days. We couldn't be happier with the amazing images.

Pip Cooper, you are a godsend. We love you more than words. You not only make everything look beautiful, you make everyone feel beautiful. Everything you brought to the images reflects us in every way, and we couldn't be more grateful. You are the best friend we could have and we are so lucky that you said yes on both books.

Thank you Alisa at Untitled Flowers for always showing up with the most beautiful flowers for all our shoots.

Thank you to Michael Istead of The Herball, for sharing your recipe with us.

To Rebecca Kaplan, Michael Sand and their team at Abrams. We are honoured and excited to be published by you in America.

To all our foreign publishers – we are so happy to have our words and thoughts translated into so many languages, thank you. And huge thanks to Khan Lawrence and Catherine Turner who have sold our book around the world.

To all of you that have supported our first book – we are blown away daily by your comments, pictures and emails. And we hope you like this one as much!

To Casey, Jonah and Huxley – you make us want to create more rituals and memories in life.

ABOUT THE AUTHORS

Nadia Narain is one of the Europe's top yoga teachers, known for her range of bestselling DVDs. She began her career teaching yoga on tour with bands, and then became one of the original teachers at London's celebrated Triyoga centre. She has her own range of chemical-free candles and perfume.

[O] @nadianarain

Katia Narain Phillips has worked in wellness, food and massage for more than twenty years. Hailed as a 'health-food pioneer' by *Red* magazine, she opened a raw food café over ten years ago, and now runs the innovative Nectar Café in London. She lives in London with her husband and her two sons.

[O] @katianarainphillips

Nadia and Katia's first book, *Self-Care for the Real World*, was a top ten bestseller in the United Kingdom and has been translated into six languages.

[O] @nadia.and.katia

PICTURE CREDITS

Photograph on page 18 © Austin Lord/Stocksy United.

Photograph on page 53 © Alita Ong/Stocksy United.

All other photographs © Issy Croker 2018.

1 3 5 7 9 10 8 6 4 2

Hutchinson
20 Vauxhall Bridge Road
London SW1V 2SA

Hutchinson is part of the Penguin Random House group of companies whose
addresses can be found at global.penguinrandomhouse.com

For photography copyright and acknowledgements see page 191.

First published in the United Kingdom by Hutchinson in 2018

www.penguin.co.uk

A CIP catalogue record for this book is available from the British Library.

ISBN 978-1786331571

Design by HART STUDIO

Printed and bound in Italy by L.E.G.O. S.p.A.

Penguin Random House is committed to a sustainable future for our business, our
readers and our planet. This book is made from Forest Stewardship Council®
certified paper.